A Hawksmere Report

SUCCESSFUL COMPETITIVE TENDERING

Jeff Woodhams

HAWKSMERE

Other Hawksmere Reports:

**Implementing
e-procurement**
Eric Evans and
Maureen Reason

**Understanding
SMART Procurement
in the MoD**
Tim Boyce

**Techniques of
Structuring and
Drafting Commercial
Contracts**
Robert Ribeiro

**Strategic Planning in
Public Relations**
Kieran Knights

**Knowledge
Management**
Sue Brelade and
Chris Harman

**The Internet and
e-commerce**
Peter Carey

**Selling Skills for
Professionals**
Kim Tasso

Published by Hawksmere plc
12-18 Grosvenor Gardens
London SW1W 0DH.
www.hawksmere.co.uk

A CIP catalogue record for this Report
is available from the British Library.

ISBN 1 85418 235 8

Printed in Great Britain by printflow.com

The author

Jeff Woodhams, MA, ACIS, MCIPS, MIMgt is an experienced commercial consultant and specialist in European Directives. He is an advocate of achieving value for money through the use of well trained staff and new technology.

He specialises in all aspects of procurement, contract law, licensing and royalties, tender assessment, computer systems and state of the art technology, as well as providing 'Red Team' consultancy to clients preparing critical tenders. He is Chairman of the EDIFACT Message Development Group overseeing electronic trading between purchasers and suppliers and Chairman of EEG12, the European Public Procurement Message Development Group as well as EU Director of the EU-China Joint Public Procurement Project and an International Expert on the Asian Development Bank Project on the Implementation of The Bidding Law and Related Regulations in the People's Republic of China.

Before becoming a consultant to the electrical supply industry and other industries and public bodies he was Head of Staff Support, Group Procurement Department in the National Grid Company. His responsibilities included the implementation and development of procurement procedures, forms of contract, contractual conditions and terms, vendor evaluation, procurement training, trade association support and the implications of the completion of the Single European Market.

After starting his career in various parts of the electricity supply industry, he moved on to CEGB Transmission Division in 1982 as Principal Contracts Officer (Plant). In 1988 he was appointed Head of Commercial Services in CEGBs Procurement Department.

Contents

1 THE COMMERCIAL CONTEXT 2

2 HOW EUROPEAN RULES CAN HELP YOU 17

3 THE BIDDING DECISION 22

4 PREQUALIFICATION 31

5 PLANNING AND ORGANISING FOR THE TENDER 35

6
PRICING AND RISK MANAGEMENT
43

7
WRITING YOUR TENDER
59

8 PUTTING YOUR TENDER TOGETHER 69

9 PRESENTATIONS AND REVIEW 82

10 THE LEGAL ISSUES 94

11 ELECTRONIC TENDERING 104

12 PERFECT YOUR TENDERS 108

APPENDICES 116

Introduction

The aim of this Report is to help you become more successful in your tendering. If you follow the suggestions and instructions contained within you should see your success rate rise. The Report is aimed at leading you towards winning successful contracts. It does not rely on 'tricks' to win the bidding process. It is written with the knowledge that you or your organisation will have to perform the contracts that you gain. You will succeed when these contracts are profitable to you, when your customers are delighted with the performance of the contract and when you deliver what they want, on time, and at the cost they expect to pay. Success is not about winning contracts at any price – success is about the long-term prosperity of your organisation.

I hope that you enjoy the following pages and that you find some suggestions which will improve your success at tendering.

Jeff Woodhams

The commercial context

chapter 1

Chapter 1:
The commercial context

The competitive environment

Tenders feature in any organisation that gains business from the outside world. They form a key role in the sales effort and for many companies become the primary selling documents.

Tenders often form the basis of the legal relationship between the seller and purchaser and the promises made in them are enforceable by law. They are often written in a hurry and are sometimes issued without being checked or properly authorised and are often presented in a very poor way. All this is unnecessary. The right planning and controls, together with proper preparation, will overcome all these common weaknesses and produce better tenders, which mean improved business.

In the distant past the majority of contracts were based on oral promises between the parties. As more people learned to write, these promises started to be written down, and the modern tender is an evolution from this process. A written document helps you retain control, communicate what you believe you are providing clearly and unambiguously, and helps you protect yourself from the purchaser demanding things which you never intended to provide.

Increasingly, customers have less expertise than they used to and they look to their bidders to make proposals as to how their problem should be solved. This gives bidders greater freedom to play on their strengths in providing goods or services, but it can also involve considerable work. There is a very fine dividing line between submitting a proposal and giving free consultancy. Some clients now find that they have to pay for tenders because they have abused bidders' trust. Bidders do want one of their number to be awarded a contract and one of the most frustrating aspects of tendering is finding that no work for anyone results from all the hard work put into preparing tenders.

Interestingly, many organisations now find themselves working in various forms of partnering arrangements with both their customers and their suppliers. Partnering is based on trust and in the most extreme forms the agreement is verbal only, with nothing in writing. We have therefore returned to the earliest form of contract – oral promises. However, nearly all partnering starts with a competitive tendering exercise and the arrangement will be tested for continuing value for money, again usually by tendering.

What is the customer's procurement process?

In the past it was normal for purchasers, especially larger ones, to issue enquiry documentation that went into great detail. Contractors were told specifically how to carry out a process or make an item of plant, and really could only answer 'yes' or 'no' to the demands of the purchaser. In terms of technical expertise, the purchaser knew as much about what was needed as the supplier, if not more. The purchaser used their knowledge to produce a detailed specification and the supplier simply had to quote to supply the parts listed.

Suppliers and contractors have now become experts in their own field and have been required to contribute more and more to the design or specification, and their submissions have become more substantial as a result. They have had to demonstrate that they can manage the whole task and so quotations have evolved into tenders and proposals.

Purchasers are now seeking longer-term relationships with their suppliers and relying more heavily on their suppliers as they concentrate on their 'core' business. Suppliers therefore have to be more imaginative to be chosen by the purchaser. Purchasers are no longer the expert, at least not in all areas of their business, and they are therefore having to buy in expertise. This means that their contractors and suppliers are expected to take a share of the risk in the project in return for becoming an essential part of the supply chain.

Planning

It is the eternal hope of purchasing managers that an accurate plan will be produced which will enable them to work on a contract strategy in good time, to obtain the best value for money. However, this is rarely achieved, often for very good reasons, and enquiries are issued in a rush. The EEC is adding pressure to all public sector bodies and utilities to plan their requirements better. Purchasers would also like to be able to issue their enquiries in an even pattern over the year, but again this is usually thwarted by the pattern of activity in the relevant sector. You may also like to see a greater spread of tendering activity and sometimes suppliers talk about offering purchasers incentives for undertaking work at off-peak times of the year. My experience is that this has never come to anything because suppliers totally underestimate the size of the pricing advantage that must be offered to overcome the increased costs incurred by the purchaser. This has to be at least 20% to stand a remote chance of being considered.

Purchasers in the public and utility sectors are supposed to publish notices in the *Official Journal of the European Communities* setting out their procurement plans over the next twelve months. Those contractors and suppliers in a partnership relationship with their customers should receive early warning about future requirements.

Vendor evaluation or qualification

Many utilities have operated vendor evaluation systems for many years and now the EEC is giving them further impetus. Local authorities have buying guides and central Government registers of contractors. Many private sector purchasers have lists of approved tenderers. Some European countries also have national lists, particularly for civil engineering and building contractors. If a purchaser operates such a system it is essential that potential tenderers apply to go onto it. Contractors and suppliers will be sent a questionnaire to complete and they may have to receive visits from the purchaser's technical or quality experts. It is important that companies treat these seriously. I have seen recent examples where a supplier omitted even to state what he was prepared to supply, presumably on the grounds that his customers knew this already. However, this is a dangerous assumption and with increased competition around any potential tenderer who does not abide by the purchaser's rules will be at a disadvantage and may not be asked to submit a proposal again.

The likelihood is that the majority of applicants will be approved onto a vendor qualification system. The information you supply, along with the purchaser's experience of dealing with you, will determine how often a proposal is sought from you.

Tender list approval

Call for competition

If the purchaser is subject to the EC procurement directives they will need to issue a call for competition. This is the case even in areas where they feel they have a special relationship with the purchaser. The purchaser must then consider all those who express an interest in supplying the goods, work or services required.

Multiple inputs

In order to be selected to receive an enquiry tenderers must overcome a number of hurdles. The likelihood is that technical, commercial and quality staff will all have a say on who does or does not get invited to tender. Tenderers must therefore satisfy a number of individuals, departments or sections before they receive an enquiry.

Refinement of vendor evaluation data

It is quite normal for purchasers to require an update of the data they hold on any vendor evaluation system as they prepare a tender list. Because time will be limited, tenderers must respond promptly to any such requests they receive.

Enquiry

If an enquiry is issued tenderers have only a limited time in which to put their proposal together.

Requests for further information

If you as a tenderer require further information or clarification from the purchaser make sure you request this in good time. The purchaser may need to consider the answer and the European directives prevent them from issuing new or additional information within six days of the tender return date. Any extra information sent out by the purchaser should be sent to all tenderers and some will also send out a complete list of all questions asked and the answers given.

Site visits

Many purchasers offer the chance of a site visit during the tender period and it would be foolish to ignore this. If the purchaser feels tenderers should visit the site, accept their judgement. If you do not, you may miss some vital information (e.g. restricted access, poor ground conditions, and safety restrictions) which you will be deemed to have taken into account anyway.

Receipt of proposals

Nearly all utilities and authorities will arrange for all tenders and proposals to be held securely on receipt and kept unopened until the due date and time. There will be a time limit for receipt and you must ensure your tender arrives on the purchaser's premises by that time.

Opening of proposals

Tenders to utilities and the private sector will be opened in private and usually all at the same time, except that turning a proposal into a contract may be an iterative process, with different suggestions being considered at different times. Some tenders to public authorities will, however, be subject to public opening. Purchasers will take into account the information supplied as part of the proposal, but may disregard any supplementary information supplied later, unless this is in response to their own questions.

Late tenders

Because purchasers wish to treat all tenderers equally, late tenders present them with a real problem in case prices have got out and the late tenderer therefore has an advantage. Purchasers will normally only consider a late tender if there is evidence that the tender was posted on time – this requires a legible Royal Mail frank – company franking machine dates are not good enough. Tenderers who expect to need more time to prepare their bid must ask for an extension to the tendering period well in advance. This may or may not be given. If not and if the tenderer cannot complete the tender on time, then the invitation should be declined. Do not simply fail to return a tender as this will count against your inclusion on future tender lists. Note that under the European directives purchasers may have to stick to the originally declared return date – it is unclear whether extensions are permissible.

Confidentiality

All proposals should be treated as confidential and in return purchasers will expect you to keep their requirements confidential. Any special requirements will be spelt out and must be adhered to. In particular, you will be in trouble if you discuss your proposal with other tenderers. However, you are likely to be presenting your ideas for solving the purchaser's problem and you will need to protect your intellectual property, especially if you do not win a contract as a result.

Purchasing policies

The purchaser has to decide on an appropriate form of contract. However, with a proposal you have the chance to influence the choice made.

Types of contract

Different types of contract offer differing degrees of risk to the purchaser and the contractor. For certain types of work, particular forms of contract are normally used, and any change to the standard practice needs to be thought through and discussed with potential customers in order to get the best deal.

Definite work

This form of contract provides the least risk to the purchaser and the most risk to the contractor, in the form of price. Once a proposal has been accepted the purchaser knows how much they will be paying (provided, of course, they do not change their mind during the contract). However, this form of contract takes

time and money for the contractor to produce a proposal, and as contractors' costs all get passed back to purchasers in the price, it can increase the costs faced by purchasers if used inappropriately. For this form of contract to work successfully, the purchaser must know what they want in sufficient detail, this will enable them to produce a clear and exact specification, covering all the unknown factors adequately (such as ground conditions). If this information is not provided, tenderers will inflate their prices to allow for their increased risk.

This form of contract cannot be used for emergency work, unless suitable provision for this has been made in advance.

On larger projects lasting several years, purchasers may allow inflation adjustment by means of a contract price adjustment formula, although part of the price will remain fixed. With reducing inflation and price regulation purchasers are looking for ever longer fixed price periods – anything up to five years may be sought.

Part definite/part remeasure

This next form of contract is a hybrid, where the work that can be specified in sufficient detail is subject to a lump sum, while the work that is not known in detail is subject to a more flexible form of contract (one of the following).

Bills of quantities

Here, various tasks are priced by the tenderers against estimated quantities provided by the purchaser. The individual prices are multiplied by the quantities to produce an overall sum. This form is traditionally used for civil engineering and building contracts, as it allows the architect or consultant engineer to work on and refine the design while the contract is proceeding. However, there is usually a need to agree 'star' rates, which are prices for tasks or items that were not originally covered. Tenderers often attempt to load their prices so that they recoup the maximum amount of payment as early as possible and they will also be looking for items which the purchaser has under quantified, so that they will try to end up with a higher contract price than the original tender sum.

Schedule of rates

This next form of contract is very similar to bills of quantities, in that individual tasks or items are priced in the tender, but with this form no estimated quantity is provided. Sometimes, tenderers are asked to include their estimate of what the total sum will be, but it is vital that tenders are assessed on the basis of common quantities. This form is often used for work that is incidental to a mainly lump sum definite work contract.

Brand identity	Advertising	Packaging
Brochures	Marketing campaigns	Training support
Web design	Catalogues	Brand guidelines
Direct mail	E-marketing	Exhibitions
Annual reports	AV presentations	Tenders

:LPING YOU WIN MORE CONTRACTS WITH .OFESSIONAL AND CONSISTENT :ESENTATION.

look at your tenders and think 'Could the presentation be better?' 'Does it let me down?' worry – you're far from alone.

.king to our clients we've found that the pressures of tight deadlines and tight budgets mean .ll to often the way the tender is presented just isn't considered. And that's a problem when ¡ cost as much as 10% of the value of the contract to put the proposal together – meaning thousands of pounds.

·hat can you do to make the presentation of your tenders live up to the .ent you've so carefully prepared?

here to find out how we can help present your tender for you, or follow these steps to ·ce the best result possible:

·et more from the time available

·tender will have to be submitted at a fixed time, and you will probably be working on the .s of it until the last minute – but you can still make maximum use of the time that is ·ble.

Right at the start, plan how you will present the tender, and while the detail is being finalised, make sure someone is preparing that presentation
Use a format that lets details be added or amended at the last minute:
   o Folders
   o Wiro bound documents
   o Ring binders
   o PDFs on CD
Settle on a design for your tender – this can be being produced while you are preparing the detail and will help you structure the final documents.
Produce a template for your Word documents. This will make sure all your documents look professional – and save your team time.
Get someone proof-reading your documents – even if 20% of it changes – you can at least be sure the other 80% is right.

·epare for next time

·think you don't have time for your team to do anything with your current tender – check with ·esigners to see if there is anything they can achieve in the timescale.

·f they can't help, you can start preparing for the next tender.

Look for the common elements from this tender that can be used again for the next one and then make sure they're right.
Plan now how you want your presentation to look – not when you're up against it when the next tender comes in.

·t advice

.l as making sure that your Tender looks professional and consistent, there are obviously more to consider to make sure you win the business.

·r Tender Heath Check and presentation ideas and examples to see for yourself whether your r Presentations are up to scratch.

·t help

NO-OBLIGATION TENDER ASSESSMENT

here to help. Although we can't advise you on the business information in your tenders, we

SET YOUR TENDER PRESENTATIONS APART:
Here are some examples of how we can help you.

Tender health check

Powerpoint

Examples

GET IN TOUCH
T: 01509 22 44 66
E: CREATIVE@HULLABALOO.CO.UK

JOIN OUR MAILING LIST >

Hullabaloo are a full-service design company, we also offer the following:

Brand identity

Brochures

Web design

Direct mail

Annual reports

Advertising

Marketing campaigns

Catalogues

E-marketing

AV presentations

Packaging

Training support

Brand guidelines

Exhibitions

Tenders

...ssess your current proposals and provide feedback on how the presentation of it could be ...oved – all with absolutely no obligation. This will cover both the use of language (ie the way ...ender is written and structured) and the way it looks.

... with many other corporate visual communications, we help our clients produce cost effective ...ighly professional tender presentations - quickly, simply and with minimum effort on your

...an tailor our solutions to fit each tender, and every budget – and measured in relation to the ... of the contract, the small investment in the presentation really does go a long way.

...ullabaloo we offer a full tender presentation service that typically falls ...one of these 4 options:

...ion 1 – lowest cost
...roduce all the contents of your tender, and we create the folders, dividers, title pages, ...nts pages, CDs – even a presentation box that the tender will be contained in – all the ...sing' to give your tender a professional appearance.

...ion 2 – low cost
...reate a Microsoft Word template you can use to produce all the content of the tender. This ...es you to simply select from pre-determined style sheets to apply Heading, Chapter Heading, ...etc to the content of your tender. So even if several different people are independently ...ing on different documents, they will all have a consistent style. Combined with Option 1 this ...ive a highly professional look to your tender.

...ion 3 – higher cost but less required from you
...and over the written tender to us and we produce the whole thing for you a section at a time, ...ng sure the whole thing looks professional – and leaving you free to spend the time you would ...used 'tidying up your presentation' to make sure the content is exactly right.

...on 4 – any of the above PLUS additional support in writing your tender
...an't tell you what to say in your tender, but if you need support writing it we can take your ...ment and use our network of copywriters to check the way it is written and the language used ...ke sure it is easy to read, and grammatically correct.

...IN TOUCH
...iscuss your tender call Jay on 01509 224466 or email ...tive@hullabaloo.co.uk.

...OUR MAILING LIST
...free helpful tools and tips or simply just learn more about our products ...services. Click here to join now.

...o top

hullabaloo ✳
VISUAL COMMUNICATIONS

Brand identity	Advertising	Packaging
Brochures	Marketing campaigns	Training support
Web design	Catalogues	Brand guidelines
Direct mail	E-marketing	Exhibitions
Annual reports	AV presentations	Tenders

ELPING YOU WIN MORE CONTRACTS WITH OFESSIONAL AND CONSISTENT ESENTATION.

look at your tenders and think 'Could the presentation be better?' 'Does it let me down?' worry – you're far from alone.

king to our clients we've found that the pressures of tight deadlines and tight budgets mean ll to often the way the tender is presented just isn't considered. And that's a problem when cost as much as 10% of the value of the contract to put the proposal together – meaning thousands of pounds.

hat can you do to make the presentation of your tenders live up to the ent you've so carefully prepared?

here to find out how we can help present your tender for you, or follow these steps to ce the best result possible:

et more from the time available

tender will have to be submitted at a fixed time, and you will probably be working on the s of it until the last minute – but you can still make maximum use of the time that is ble.

Right at the start, plan how you will present the tender, and while the detail is being finalised, make sure someone is preparing that presentation
Use a format that lets details be added or amended at the last minute:
  o Folders
  o Wiro bound documents
  o Ring binders
  o PDFs on CD
Settle on a design for your tender – this can be being produced while you are preparing the detail and will help you structure the final documents.
Produce a template for your Word documents. This will make sure all your documents look professional – and save your team time.
Get someone proof-reading your documents – even if 20% of it changes – you can at least be sure the other 80% is right.

epare for next time

think you don't have time for your team to do anything with your current tender – check with esigners to see if there is anything they can achieve in the timescale.

f they can't help, you can start preparing for the next tender.

Look for the common elements from this tender that can be used again for the next one and then make sure they're right.
Plan now how you want your presentation to look – not when you're up against it when the next tender comes in.

t advice

l as making sure that your Tender looks professional and consistent, there are obviously more to consider to make sure you win the business.

r Tender Heath Check and presentation ideas and examples to see for yourself whether your Presentations are up to scratch.

t help

NO-OBLIGATION TENDER ASSESSMENT

here to help. Although we can't advise you on the business information in your tenders, we

---

SET YOUR TENDER PRESENTATIONS APART:
Here are some examples of how we can help you.

Tender health check

Powerpoint

Examples

GET IN TOUCH
T: 01509 22 44 66
E: CREATIVE@HULLABALOO.CO.UK

JOIN OUR MAILING LIST >

Hullabaloo are a full-service design company, we also offer the following:

Brand identity

Brochures

Web design

Direct mail

Annual reports

Advertising

Marketing campaigns

Catalogues

E-marketing

AV presentations

Packaging

Training support

Brand guidelines

Exhibitions

Tenders

assess your current proposals and provide feedback on how the presentation of it could be improved – all with absolutely no obligation. This will cover both the use of language (ie the way tender is written and structured) and the way it looks.

As with many other corporate visual communications, we help our clients produce cost effective highly professional tender presentations - quickly, simply and with minimum effort on your

can tailor our solutions to fit each tender, and every budget – and measured in relation to the of the contract, the small investment in the presentation really does go a long way.

Hullabaloo we offer a full tender presentation service that typically falls one of these 4 options:

ion 1 – lowest cost
produce all the contents of your tender, and we create the folders, dividers, title pages, nts pages, CDs – even a presentation box that the tender will be contained in – all the sing' to give your tender a professional appearance.

on 2 – low cost
create a Microsoft Word template you can use to produce all the content of the tender. This es you to simply select from pre-determined style sheets to apply Heading, Chapter Heading, etc to the content of your tender. So even if several different people are independently ng on different documents, they will all have a consistent style. Combined with Option 1 this ive a highly professional look to your tender.

on 3 – higher cost but less required from you
and over the written tender to us and we produce the whole thing for you a section at a time, g sure the whole thing looks professional – and leaving you free to spend the time you would used 'tidying up your presentation' to make sure the content is exactly right.

on 4 – any of the above PLUS additional support in writing your tender
an't tell you what to say in your tender, but if you need support writing it we can take your nent and use our network of copywriters to check the way it is written and the language used ke sure it is easy to read, and grammatically correct.

IN TOUCH
iscuss your tender call Jay on 01509 224466 or email tive@hullabaloo.co.uk.

OUR MAILING LIST
free helpful tools and tips or simply just learn more about our products services. Click here to join now.

o top

Google Search

Articles For Authors
bmit Articles
embers Login
nefits
pert Authors
ad Endorsements
itorial Guidelines
thor TOS

For Publishers
rms of Service
nes / Email Alerts
nage Subscriptions
neArticles RSS

For Everyone
bg
rums
out Us
ntact Us
cicle Writing Shop
vertising
iliates
vacy Policy
e Map

rch EzineArticles

Search
Advanced Search

HOME::Writing-and-Speaking/Writing

How To Write A Winning Tender
By Azhar Victor ☆

Article Word Count: 417   [View Summary] Comments (0)

🖨 **Print This Article**
📄 **EzinePublisher**
📧 **Send To Friends**
⭐ **Add To Favorites**
💬 **Post A Comment**
▼ **Suggest Topic**
↓ **Report Article**

A Business Opportunity

How to write a winning tender is a question which would be uppermost in the minds of most business executives and entrepreneurs looking at new business opportunities. Bidding for a tender is one way of offering to provide your products and services to a potential customer. The tender document would include details of what exactly is the product or service required, quantity, price and other specifications as well as conditions. The offer or bid would be a response to meeting the specifications and conditions stipulated in the tender document. More importantly, the bid should be how and why an organization or party should be awarded the contract or job. It must be borne in mind, that the bid usually takes place in a very competitive business environment. Therefore, the written bid must be prepared in a careful and thoughtful manner.

Content Outline

- In writing a winning tender, it is important that it begins with a summary of the key specifications and conditions listed and how these would be met. Is there any differentiating factor in your bid? This could be your hands-on approach or personal ownership of all jobs awarded to your organization or company.
- State how and why you qualify for the job. Leverage on your team's professional qualifications, experiences, previous bids awarded, successful completion and customer satisfaction.
- Focus on what is most important to the customer. Is it on timely completion, price, quality or a combination of these and several other criteria? Address them with an assurance of fulfillment.
- What are your plans for managing the job or project? Delivery schedules and project completion timelines would be helpful.
- Explain how you would be able to add value to the job if you are successful and identify any mutually beneficial outcomes.

General Guidelines

Ensure that the written tender is a comprehensive and complete document particularly in terms of the specifications and conditions listed in the tender. Check and re-check for compliance. Include a cover letter which would make a crucial first impression. Provide a listing of the contents of your document and on how it has been organized for easy reference. The document must be written such that it is easy to read. Check spelling and grammar. Where required, obtain the services or assistance of others who have specialized writing skills. You can now even use software for editing your written work. It is worth the effort.

Should you need to use software to enable you to write better, you will find this site useful.

Do you wish you could translate ideas into words the way you think it? There is now available a writing software which does this for you. It uses a unique technology to provide the first context-related, all-in-one solution for improving writing. Developed by a leading team of

software, algorithm, and Natural Language Processing experts, for the first time ever, users can easily enhance their writing skills. This revolutionary writing tool instantly analyzes the complete text and provides context-based recommendations to replace words with synonyms, to add adjectives and adverbs, to check spelling, and to verify proper use of grammar.

Learn more here.

Article Source: http://EzineArticles.com/?expert=Azhar_Victor

Other Recent EzineArticles from the Writing-and-Speaking:Writing Category:

- Writing When You Are Excited
- How to Write a Scary Story - Some Frightening Tips
- Topic Sentences
- 5 Writing Mistakes to Avoid
- My Tryst With the Online Freelancing World
- Writing Tip - Stopping Readers in Their Tracks
- How to Choose a Bestselling Book Title - Part 2
- How a Bestselling Book Title Can Skyrocket Your Sales
- Deadly Mistakes With Agents & Publishers - Part 1
- How to Sell 100 Million Books
- Relax, Get Inspired and Start Writing
- Researching "Eagle Rising"
- Writing by Using Both Sides of the Brain
- Home Writing Jobs - Fantasy Or Reality?
- Arts and Crafts Business Plan (Key Writing Elements)

Most Viewed EzineArticles in the Writing-and-Speaking:Writing Category (90 Days)

1. Hook Your Reader With the Very First Sentence
2. How to Start Writing a Book - Checklist of Top 5 Ways to Write Your Novel Like a Pro
3. Thank You Appreciation Verses - Unique Examples For Your Cards and Notes
4. Fiction Writing Tips - 6 Golden Rules For Fiction Writers
5. Best Types of Writing Worksheet
6. Characters - How to Make Your Reader Love Your Villain
7. How to Become a Great Writer
8. Quitting Your Job? Here's How to Write a Resignation Letter You Won't Regret
9. How to End Your Story
10. Simple Ways to Improve Your Creative Writing
11. Achieving Maximum Writing Results - Rely on Descriptive Word Lists
12. 7 Tips on How to Write a Book
13. How to Write a Brochure
14. How to Write a Formal RSVP to an Invitation
15. What to Do When You Think Your Writing Stinks

Most Published EzineArticles in the Writing-and-Speaking:Writing Category

1. How to Start Writing a Book - Checklist of Top 5 Ways to Write Your Novel Like a Pro
2. Fiction Writing Tips - 6 Golden Rules For Fiction Writers
3. Convert Your Knowledge Into an Extra Income
4. How to Write a Book the Easy Way
5. Writing Tips - Learn From Great Children's Book Writers & Illustrators
6. Five Tips For Writing a Cartoon Screenplay
7. Writing That Gets Results
8. Simple Ways to Improve Your Creative Writing
9. How to Become a Great Writer
10. Hook Your Reader With the Very First Sentence
11. Characters - How to Make Your Reader Love Your Villain
12. If You're a Children's Writer, You Need a Blog!
13. Writing Discipline Comes With Practice, Practice, Practice
14. How to Beat Writer's Block and Write Your Book
15. Freelance Writing For Beginners - 3 Tips

- APA Style Citation:
  Victor, A. (2008, February 7). *How To Write A Winning Tender*. Retrieved May 22, 2009, from
  http://ezinearticles.com/?How-To-Write-A-Winning-Tender&id=971969

- Chicago Style Citation:
  Victor, Azhar "How To Write A Winning Tender." *How To Write A Winning Tender EzineArticles.com*.
  http://ezinearticles.com/?How-To-Write-A-Winning-Tender&id=971969

A Four Step Approach to Successful Tenders & Sales Presentations

ne
vices
nts
e Fact Sheets & Advice
sletter
tact Us
ut Second Opinion

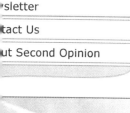

A Four Step Approach to Successful Tenders & Sales Presentations

Happy New Year to all Practical Marketing readers. Hopefully you managed some time for rest, relaxation and even a little bit of business planning during the seasonal break. If you did the latter perhaps you reviewed your success rates in securing new business – from tenders, quotes, sales presentation? If you haven't looked at these ratios recently maybe the start of a new year is a good time to do so.

Perhaps you'll be one of the lucky few who can report exceptional results – but most of us, when we look at our success rates, would like to see improvements in the number of proposals we manage to convert to actual business.

This 4 step approach is intended to supply some pointers and ideas for those who'd like to be more successful in tendering for new business and making sales presentations.

Step 1 – Research and explore

This stage is critical in making sure your proposal or sales pitch pushes all the right buttons and makes your prospective customer or client want to buy from you.

No matter what business you are pitching for you'll have some information about your prospective client. Who are they, where are they, what business they are in? You should also make it your business to find out more – who are their customers? Why are they willing to consider an approach from you? Who do they buy from at the moment?

In this stage your goal is to create a very clear picture of what makes your prospective client tick, what's important to them, what problems they face, who the decision makers are and the needs they have in their business that you might be able to satisfy?

If you can really get under their skin and understand what keeps them awake at night you're in a good position to present a proposition to them that they'll find difficult to resist.

Step 2 – Write or prepare your argument

This is possibly the most difficult stage and one we're all probably guilty of putting off – sometimes for the right reasons (we want to make sure we've gathered all the relevant information about our prospect and are clear which approach will be most appealing) but all too often for the wrong reasons (we don't know where to start, are worried we won't get it anyway or think we can dash something off in half an hour immediately before the deadline)

By having a clear structure you can overcome the initial problem – this might also help you to realise a rushed response just won't do.

A simple suggested structure is as follows;

1. Title
    make it punchy and use it to show what solution/ advantage you will deliver.

2. Needs

restate your prospective client's needs or requirements.

3. Solution
briefly explain what you'll deliver – make sure this section is full of benefits and pay back.

4. Why choose us?
provide brief credentials, only use things relevant to this prospective client.

5. Budget
include a clearly set out quote. Don't hide anything. Provide sufficient information for them to make a decision.

6. Summary
depending how long the proposal is this might be an executive summary at the start or could be a brief, punchy paragraph at the end of the proposal.

7. Close
do so by saying you want the business and leave doors open for them to contact you.

If you follow this structure you can't go far wrong.

In addition to structure you do need to make sure that the content is appropriate – avoid jargon (unless this helps show how well you understand this business) Write in brief, well constructed sentences and edit down to the essentials. Most proposals are read by busy executives or managers – lengthy proposals tend to be left until last and judged against shorter/earlier read ones. Use bullets and headings selectively to highlight your main points.

All of these points apply whether you are preparing a written proposal or some kind of sales presentation.

Step 3 – Review or rehearse
Having produced a first draft of your proposal re-read and edit – preferably also asking someone else to read for you, to spot inconsistencies, typos and to confirm whether you have really addresses all the critical needs of your clients (as stated in the first section of your proposal).

One of the reasons for discussing 11th hour proposal writing, mentioned in Step 2, is ideally you should leave the proposal for a few a days and re-read – again checking you are hitting all the right notes and meeting their requirements.

If you're presenting your proposal in person do rehearse preferably with a constructively critical audience. And always bear in mind your audience may, and you should hope will, ask questions. You should try and encourage questions since this enables you to develop rapport and the nature of their questions can give clues to their real areas of interests, concerns or true needs.

Step 4 – Send and follow up
This ought to be the most straight forward of processes really but too often it is not executed effectively. A written proposal nowadays is often accepted by email but if you are producing a printed copy then do take some time over its production – bind a lengthy proposal and add page numbers and an index, print out in colour if you are using diagrams or charts – or even for the benefit of your logo.

And whether you are sending electronically or in hard copy always include a covering message (in the email or in a covering letter). If appropriate summarise any critical points from your proposal, for example when you're available to start the work or when you could deliver the product and don't forget to ask for the work again – phrases like 'we would very much like to work with you on this important project' or 'we are really keen to start supplying you with our product' are OK –

provided you mean it and everything about your proposal has demonstrated that you want their business and will provide the quality and service they demand.

Your covering message should always mention that you will follow up (not assume that they'll call you!) And then make sure you do follow up – make the call when you said you would and always leave the door open for a future contact, even if you're not successful this time.

And the follow up call is a great time to get feedback – positive or negative – on your approach, the solution, costs – just about every aspect. Don't be afraid to ask – most people will give honest feedback – and you can learn from that.

Article written by Teresa Harris, Second Opinion Marketing. Teresa is an independent marketing consultant specialising in communication solutions and the customer experience. To contact Second Opinion Marketing call 01789 740396 or email tah@secondopinionmarketing.co.uk.

To subscribe to practical marketing and receive articles like this one free to your in box each month subscribe today.

For more ideas, tips and articles click here.

Useful links

Institute of Sales and Marketing
Chartered Institute of Marketing

Designed by Zarr

Business
Link

Tender for a contract

Submitting a tender is common for businesses supplying goods or services to other businesses or the public sector.

At a basic level you expect to **quote** for a job or write a letter saying why you should be given the business.

More **formal tenders** often apply to bigger jobs or for supply contracts spread over time. Public-sector work in particular has specific tendering processes. This applies to customers ranging from your local council or hospital to a central government department.

Even if you don't win the work this time, writing a tender can clarify your aims, strengths and weaknesses and you can learn for next time by asking for feedback on your bid. It raises your profile with the customer and helps you learn about customers' needs.

This guide explains how to identify potential contracts, what to include in your tender and how to write it for the best chance of success.

Finding out about contracts

You can find out about **private-sector contracts** in a number of ways:

- build contacts with potential customers
- advertise in local and national newspapers
- advertise in trade and professional magazines covering your area of business
- research contracts outside your business sector which may produce secondary contracts for you, eg if a new office block is built, it will need desks, carpets, signage, stationery, cleaning and laundry
- follow up press and other reports - a company may be expanding or sub-contracting part of a big order
- network and pick up information from other businesses

You can identify **public-sector contracts** by:

- following up contract notices published in newspapers and trade magazines
- monitoring online government tender notices - find information about government contracts on the Supply2.gov.uk website (registration required) - Opens in a new window
- searching free for 'above threshold' contracts (with a value that exceeds the threshold above which an invitation to tender must be published throughout the European Union (EU) - you can search for 'above threshold' contracts on the Tenders Electronic Daily (TED) website (registration required) - Opens in a new window
- contact your local Enterprise Europe Network on the Enterprise Europe Network website - Opens in a new window

You can find information on non-EU public sector contracts on the UK Trade & Investment website (registration required) - Opens in a new window.

You can download a guide to tendering for public contracts from the Department for Business, Enterprise and Regulatory Reform (BERR) website (PDF) - Opens in a new window or you can order a copy from the BERR Publications Unit Order Line on Tel **0845 015 0010** .

Should you bid for a tender?

Preparing tenders can help you to win big orders, but it can also be time-consuming, cost money and tie up valuable resources. If you don't get the contract, the money and time spent is usually lost so carefully weigh up whether or not a tender is worth bidding for.

Key points to consider before tendering

- Get hold of the bid documents and analyse them.
- Make sure you can match the technical, skill and experience requirements.
- How much will it cost to prepare your bid?
- Would the work fit in with your strategy and positioning of your business?
- Estimate the costs of fulfilling the contract and whether or not you'd make enough money to justify it.
- Assess how the contract would affect your other work, staffing and ability to take on other new business.

You also need to consider how important the customer is to your business. Is this a good potential client or one you don't want to offend by not tendering? Try to understand things from the client's point of view.

You can download a guide to tendering for public contracts from the Department for Business, Enterprise and Regulatory Reform (BERR) website (PDF) - Opens in a new window or you can order a copy from the BERR Publications Unit Order Line on Tel **0845 015 0010** . Find contract opportunities on the Supply2.gov.uk website (registration required) - Opens in a new window.

Find out what the client wants

In order to gain a clearer understanding of a potential client's requirements, see if you can arrange a meeting or have a telephone conversation with them, before you start work on the tender. You should always raise questions by phone or email if tender documents are unclear - on anything from deadlines to how you'd get paid.

Make sure the client is serious, and that you're not there to make up the numbers or to test the market. Sometimes customers may just be fishing for ideas they'll then use for themselves. You can prevent this from happening by requesting customers to sign a non-disclosure agreement before presenting your tender. See our guide on non-disclosure agreements. But don't forget many clients genuinely want you to make a **creative contribution** and provide ideas.

If you're selling to the public sector, you can find advice on procurement practice

on the Office of Government Commerce (OGC) website - Opens in a new window.

You can download a guide to tendering for public contracts from the Department for Business, Enterprise and Regulatory Reform (BERR) website (PDF) - Opens in a new window or you can order a copy from the BERR Publications Unit Order Line on Tel   0845 015 0010   . You can find contract opportunities on the Supply2.gov.uk website (registration required) - Opens in a new window.

What to put in your tender

Make sure you match the bid specification and answer all the questions.

Summarise your bid and explain why it answers the client's needs. Write this last but put it at the beginning of your tender.

Crucial rules for your tender document

- **Focus on the client** - talk about their needs and how you can solve their problems. When you write about yourself, it's to prove you have the skills, experience and organisation to fulfil the client's requirements.
- Help the client by coming up with **ideas** - from alternative ways of doing things to how to tackle possible worries about future maintenance and staffing implications.
- If the client has provided a **qualification document**, make sure that you cover everything in the document.
- **Value for money** and not price alone decides most bids. Bring something to the work that can't be done by the client or your competitors. Emphasise business benefits, service improvements, risk reduction, low maintenance, quality, reliability, previous satisfied customers, lifetime costs, etc.
- Analyse all the cost and **pricing factors** of the contract. Don't ignore fixed costs such as pay for staff who could be working on something else.
- Consider whether to include some **protection of your information** from future disclosure under the Freedom of Information Act. You may wish to indicate which information you consider to be a 'trade secret' or is likely to prejudice your commercial interests if disclosed. You could also include a non-disclosure agreement. See our guide on non-disclosure agreements.
- **Contract management** - show you have the resources to do the work in a cost-effective way to meet the client's needs, hit deadlines and respond flexibly to changing situations.
- Show you've thought about - and can manage - potential financial, commercial and legal **risks** that could cause contract failure.
- Give details of **your team**. Emphasise strengths - CVs or tailored biographies should highlight successes with similar projects as well as qualifications and experience.

You can download a guide to tendering for public contracts from the Department for Business, Enterprise and Regulatory Reform (BERR) website (PDF) - Opens in a new window or you can order a copy from the BERR Publications Unit Order Line on Tel   0845 015 0010   .

Writing your tender

.

Once you've decided to bid, you'll need to decide how you'll manage the bid:

- Who gathers information and does research?
- Who co-ordinates all the material you need?
- Who writes the drafts?
- Who checks them?
- How will the rest of your firm's work get done?

A good starting point is to make a list of all the questions you would ask if a company was submitting a tender to provide a product or service to you.

Clients will expect you to:

- state the purpose and origin of the bid
- summarise your work as a contractor, past experience and credentials for this job
- say how you'll carry out the work, and how and when the client's aims will be achieved
- explain the benefits and value for money of your bid
- detail when and how goods and services are to be delivered, and provide a timetable
- demonstrate your team's skills, experience of similar work and their responsibilities if you win the contract
- explain how you will manage the project
- give details of your pricing and any aftercare arrangements within the price
- be practical and identify potential problems without promising what's clearly impossible for you to deliver

Include a **covering letter** that responds to the bid invitation, summarises your main message and explains how the documents are organised.

You should also be aware that information from your tender may be disclosed in the future under the Freedom of Information Act. This gives anyone, including your competitors, the general right to see information held by public authorities - including the information in your tender.

You should clearly indicate which information is commercially confidential. If the information is particularly sensitive, you might want to ask for a non-disclosure agreement. See our guide on non-disclosure agreements.

You can download a guide to tendering for public contracts from the Department for Business, Enterprise and Regulatory Reform (BERR) website (PDF) - Opens in a new window or you can order a copy from the BERR Publications Unit Order Line on Tel   **0845 015 0010**   .

Tips on editing your tender

It is well worth spending some time looking at the presentation of your tender. Here are some tips on editing and supplying your tender:

- Keep sentences and paragraphs short, punchy and businesslike.
- Use bullet points and headings to break up text.
- Decide on a typeface, layout and type size - not too small - and stick to them.
- Make sure everything is standardised. Are CVs all presented in the same way?

.

- Be careful when cutting and pasting text to make sure the format stays the same.
- Make sure you've developed a logical argument and that everything hangs together.
- Read everything again. Then get a colleague to read it - for meaning, typing mistakes and omissions.
- Use appendices for supporting additional information.
- Produce a front cover with the project title, date, name of the organisation requesting the tender, and that of your own firm.
- Include a contents page.
- Number paragraphs and provide a contents page so material can be easily located.
- Consider getting it printed and bound professionally - if hard copies have been requested rather than submission via email.

Above all, make sure the tender is delivered on time - it is unlikely that organisations will consider your tender if it arrives after the closing date. You may want to deliver it yourself, by hand, to ensure it arrives safely, or by courier for secure delivery. Alternatively, contact the organisation to check they have received it.

You can download a guide to tendering for public contracts from the Department for Business, Enterprise and Regulatory Reform (BERR) website (PDF) - Opens in a new window or you can order a copy from the BERR Publications Unit Order Line on Tel   **0845 015 0010**   .

Here's how I select and bid for tenders

Phoebe Hart

JJ Group - Opens in a new window

Phoebe's top tips:

- "Know your strengths and weaknesses before you start."
- "Have a plan for selecting tenders to go for."
- "Nominate a central co-ordinator."

The JJ Group is a full service marketing and new media agency based in Oxford. Established in 1989, the company's current clients include Volvo, British Gas and the Department for Work and Pensions. Marketing manager Phoebe Hart explains how a structured approach to tendering helps the company win new business.

What I did

Have a plan

"Two years ago we set up a dedicated team to co-ordinate tenders as part of our growth strategy. We began by reviewing recent contracts, analysing revenue versus costs. We also identified which market sectors and company types we wanted to target. It's important to be specific so you don't waste resources

- chasing tenders that don't fit overall business objectives.

"There are lots of ways to find out about contracts. As well as being members of relevant professional bodies, we monitor the trade press, attend networking events and use an online tool for tracking public sector contracts."

Allocate responsibilities

"At the outset of a tender we pick a team to work on it, balancing skills required against existing workloads. We always allocate the people who will actually work on the business if we win it, and we include their CVs in the tender document.

"We hold meetings at key stages and map critical paths so everyone knows what they have to produce and when. When several people are contributing to a document, it's also important to give one person responsibility for the final edit, or you can end up with disparate styles."

Prepare the pitch

"Our golden rule is to focus on what the client is asking for. Sometimes that's clear from their brief, but you can't afford to guess or get too carried away with your own ideas. If we have queries, we contact the client, which also helps to build a rapport before the tender document is submitted.

"Most tender briefs come with a budget to work to. We regularly benchmark ourselves against similar-sized agencies so we know our pricing is competitive.

"Tender documents will be read by several people within an organisation, each with a different perspective. We structure ours so that they're easy to read and the client can quickly reference the part they're interested in.

"If a presentation is required, we adapt and add to the original document, so we're not just re-hashing what the client has already read."

What I'd do differently

Be selective

"In the early stages, the scatter-gun approach prevailed and we wasted time and money tendering for contracts we shouldn't have considered. Nowadays we're more selective."

Understand the public sector

"When we first started bidding for public sector contracts, we didn't realise the difference in processes and timescales compared to the private sector. We now understand the level of detail required and the time we need to allocate."

Read more case studies that describe first hand how people tackle real-life challenges and opportunities.

Business Link Helpline

0845 600 9 006

Related guides on businesslink.gov.uk

Manage your personal list of starting-up tasks with our Business start-up organiser

Price your product or service

Overview of selling to government

Sales & marketing: the basics

Reach your customers effectively

Understand your competitors

Non-disclosure agreements

Know your customers' needs

Target the right people in an organisation

Price lists, estimates, quotations and tenders

Here's how having an up-to-date business plan helped my business

Here's how I identified and reached the right sales targets

Related web sites you might find useful

Buy an online course on written communications on the learndirect business website
http://www1.learndirect-business.com/?target=xpc.asp?course_id=5560%26wbt_type=course

Buy an online course on winning the contract on the learndirect business website
http://www1.learndirect-business.com/?target=xpc.asp?course_id=25000%26wbt_type=course

Find out about supplying products or services to government on the Supply2.gov.uk website (registration required)
http://www.supply2.gov.uk

Find out about tendering for government contracts on the Department for Business, Enterprise and Regulatory Reform (BERR) website
http://www.berr.gov.uk/whatwedo/enterprise/enterprisesmes/info-business-owners/procurement/page37909.html

Download a guide to tendering for public contracts from the BERR website (PDF)
http://www.berr.gov.uk/files/file39469.pdf

Search for 'above threshold' contracts on the TED website (registration required)
http://ted.europa.eu

Contact your local Enterprise Europe Network on the Enterprise Europe Network website
http://www.enterprise-europe-network.ec.europa.eu/index_en.htm

Find out about public-sector contracts located outside the EU on the UK Trade & Investment website (registration required)

https://www.uktradeinvest.gov.uk/ukti/appmanager/ukti/ourservices?
_nfls=false&_nfpb=true&_pageLabel=opportunities

Find out about government procurement practice on the Office of Government Commerce website
http://www.ogc.gov.uk/procurement.asp

You can find this guide by navigating to:
Home > Sales and marketing > Selling > Tender for a contract

Factsheet 1: Considerations of the Client!

When proposing to offer services to a prospective client. Especially a new client it is very useful to view your proposal and / or presentation purely from the perspective of that client in a critical manner. This will ensure you have prepared fully and considered all angles of their requirement. It will also ensure you are fully prepared for any objections, questions or queries they may have.

Below is a comprehensive list of considerations that will go through the mind of a client when considering a new supplier. Some of these considerations may be conscious and some unconscious, but rest assured they will be considered!

- What priority will this project receive from the supplier? How important will it be to his firm?
- Does their proposal meet the terms of reference and the intended scope of our requirements?
- Is the usual business of the supplier closely related to the proposed work?
- Do the references to past experience include activities specifically related to our requirements?
- Has the supplier been honoured by professional societies because of performance in this specific professional area?
- What reputation does the firm hold in the area of these requirements?
- Are the statements of past performance worded in a meaningful way so we can identify what work was actually performed and what results were actually achieved?
- Are their aspects of performance that indicate particular strengths and weaknesses?
- Is it clear which tasks will be assigned to specific personnel and for what amount of time?
- Are the personnel assigned to specific tasks qualified by training and experience to successfully perform the tasks?
- What assurances are made concerning the availability of personnel proposed?
- Do biographies relate specific experience of personnel to our specific needs?
- Does the proposal show the capabilities of the management to handle the size and complexity of our requirements?
- Is it clearly demonstrated that top level management will continue a high level of interest and assume responsibility for successful provision of services?
- Is the overall cost within range or our budget?
- What is the relationship between cost figures and delivery of services?

- Are the personnel costs reasonable according to the specialisms required? How are they comparable in the market place?
- Are the invoicing terms and conditions acceptable?

As the supplier being able to answer the points positively as you read through them is not enough. You need to ensure you address them during your proposal and presentations, or be prepared to answer them during any Q&A sessions.

CHAPTER 1: THE COMMERCIAL CONTEXT

Time and materials

This form of contract is very flexible in that the contractor provides various grades of labour to do whatever the purchaser or the engineer wants and they are recompensed on the time taken by the number of men used. All materials are provided on a cost plus basis. The contractor is under no pressure to keep costs down – indeed they increase their profit for every additional person-hour worked. They may therefore be tempted to try to spin jobs out for as long as possible. For this reason, time and materials contracts must be closely supervised, and are therefore resource intensive for the purchaser during the contract.

However, they can be started without a specification and in a great hurry and are often used for emergency work. They may also be used during the investigative phase of a project to produce enough information to allow a lump sum to be tendered for the bulk of the work. They are the usual forms of contract for dealing with consultants.

Cost reimbursable

This form of contract is similar to time and materials work, but is used for work off the purchaser's site which is therefore even more difficult to control. It used to be used for defence development work, but has now largely died out. The biggest drawback is that it removes all incentives from the contractor to control the contract.

Target cost

To try to overcome the difficulties of the previous form of contract, the concept of target cost was developed – here the contractor is reimbursed all their costs (which have to be carefully defined) but their profit is dependent on how cheaply they can complete the contract. An overall target cost is agreed, and the contractor and purchaser share the savings if the cost turns out to be less, while the contractor loses some of their profit if the costs turn out to be more. The actual incentive offered to the contractor is critically dependent on getting the target cost set at the correct level.

This form of contract has made a re-appearance in recent years under the guise of partnership sourcing.

Partnership sourcing

Partnership sourcing can mean a variety of ways of contracting, including the target cost method outlined above. It usually implies a commitment by both purchaser and supplier or contractor to get fully involved in each other's side of the contract or even each other's business, so as to produce a more efficient end result. The contractor is often required to open their books, in return for which they will be paid whatever the job costs. There is usually an incentive for both

sides to share any savings made, but the contractor will also have the freedom to comment on the purchaser's contribution to the end product and to suggest ways in which the end result may be achieved more cheaply. Proposals are often the mechanism for making these suggestions.

One form of partnership sourcing shows itself with 'just in time' manufacturing, where the manufacturer ceases to hold stocks of raw materials or components – instead they place themselves in the hands of their suppliers and have to trust them to deliver the required quantities at exactly the right time, to keep their factory or project going.

Terms of payment

Major purchasers have traditionally offered interim and progress payments on larger contracts, but have also required a retention until the warranty or maintenance period has finished. However, payments are being increasingly tied to usable sections of the work being completed and tenderers may have to look into financing contracts prior to completion. Again, the proposal offers an opportunity for you to submit suggested terms of payments. Purchasers do take into account when tenderers will require payments when evaluating their proposals and put a cost on the resulting finance charges. In many cases, your customer may be able to borrow money more cheaply than you and therefore the overall cost of the project or service may be reduced if they bear the financing charges.

Competitive completion

Increasingly, purchasers will set the date by which the goods can be supplied or the project completed, as a competitive element of the enquiry. In these cases, you should always find out the earliest date when the project will be of use to the purchaser, since they will not be willing to pay for an early completion which they cannot use.

Design ownership

Traditionally purchasers have wanted to take into their ownership all designs they have paid for. They may not have used those designs subsequently. If you feel you can exploit that design then it will be worth including this in your proposal to the purchaser, since in these commercial times purchasers are keen to hear about ways of increasing their future income.

Defects liability requirements

One of the biggest complaints of purchasers is that defects liability requirements are totally inadequate. Many of the changes to traditional conditions of contract concern defects provisions and purchasers are keen not to lose their entitlement to rectification of latent defects. Of course, purchasers do not expect to pay for this extension to the previous warranty provisions, so you must be clear about the costs of what you are offering before tendering. Remember that many purchasers cannot take plant out of service when a defect is suspected and they may require you to put the defect right at their convenience.

Key dates/liquidated damages

Liquidated damages often cause heated arguments between purchaser and supplier. Purchasers enter into contracts to have plant and equipment delivered for their use or to have services provided – they are not in the business of putting you out of business. Liquidated damages are seen as a way of putting pressure on you to deliver on time. In these commercial times you must expect purchasers to take liquidated damages if you are late, so you should ensure that realistic delivery dates or service levels are quoted. Having said that, if any competitor quotes a date which meets the purchaser's requirements (however unrealistic those requirements may seem) the purchaser is likely to give them a sympathetic hearing. You should also be prepared to see liquidated damages tied to performance requirements as well as programme.

Increasingly, purchasers see payment as a powerful incentive for timely completion and will tie payments to key stages of completion. All purchasers are after is to grab the attention of your senior management when things go wrong and with the ascendancy of accountants in UK industry, cash flow is a powerful weapon!

Tender documents – content and format

The four words – bids, proposals, quotations and tenders are used to describe very similar processes and documents. Various industries and businesses use these four words in their own specific ways. Meanings may be further confused when bidding into Europe or elsewhere, where English is not the native language of the purchaser, even though it is being used for the contract. However, it may be worth trying to make distinctions:

- A *Quotation* is a price or series of prices against a set of parts and is usually the sum stated at current prices. The parts may not necessarily fit together and the quotation may not help the customer decide which offer is the best for them. It is used for simple, straightforward and well-understood jobs.

- A *Tender* is a price to execute work or services or to supply goods at a fixed rate. A tender is more formal than a quotation and. is generally offered against a complete 'Invitation to Tender'. The word 'tender' often appears in legal books to describe an offer.

- A *Bid* can be considered synonymous with the word 'tender' for most circumstances. It is widely used in the oil industry. Sometimes, but by no means always the case, a bid is used to describe a document with less verbiage than a proposal or a tender.

- A *Proposal* can be synonymous with 'tender' and 'bid' but it is also used when describing an offer which has not formally been requested, as in an 'unsolicited proposal'. A proposal can put forward a course of action for consideration. It is often used when a contractor is offering to perform work for a potential customer who doesn't really know what they want and who is looking for ideas and solutions.

However, whichever word is used by the customer in their documents, they will have expectations about the responses they anticipate receiving and it is up to you to find out what those expectations are and to match them.

One of the problems, especially with proposals, is that they can be used as free consultancy by unscrupulous customers. You are anxious to present as good a picture of your organisation as possible and will try to be as helpful as possible to potential customers. However, proposals often require you to submit your ideas to the customer before they decide whether to buy from you. These ideas may well be your greatest asset. Consider an advertising agency pitching for a new campaign. The creative genius of the agency must be presented to the client without any guarantee of business, and the actual contract when obtained probably adds less value to the customer than the proposal. But the agency must rely on the

customer treating everyone fairly and not abusing the information and ideas obtained via the proposal. Customers who abuse this rule soon find it very difficult to obtain tenders. In the recent past certain Government Departments have been guilty of taking ideas from proposals and not awarding any contract at all and as a result they often now have to pay for bidders to produce proposals. You must judge each case on its merits, but always remember that under UK law a tender or proposal is your copyright, unless there is a legally binding agreement to the contrary.

Legal status

In order to make a legally binding contract in the UK there has to be an offer and an acceptance. Your proposal is your offer, but anything you say may be withdrawn at any time before it is accepted. In practice, this might make tender assessment difficult, so purchasers usually require you to hold your offer open for a limited period (typically 60 or 90 days). Some purchasers go further and require you to submit a bid bond. This guarantees that you will forfeit the amount of the bond if your bid is not available for acceptance during the stated period. However, in the West most purchasers rely on you not wanting to lose your commercial reputation.

In an ideal world it might be possible to conclude a verbal agreement without worrying about 'paperwork'. However, there is a problem with proof, especially if things are going wrong. This is why your proposal is so important. It sets out exactly what you are offering to do and what you expect your customer to do in return.

The conditions you offer are there to stop your customer taking excessive advantage of you and leaving you with little return for a lot of effort.

Protection extends to preventing your customer getting cheap credit from you and also to allowing you to define the best time when the title of the goods will pass.

Protection can cover your intellectual property rights and product liability. A well conceived tender can give you sensible cover for many liabilities. Environmental topics can also be addressed in a tender and certain aspects can be spelt out to stop undue claims being made.

Evaluating the tenders

Your customer will be involved in a lot of effort – they may have half a dozen or even a dozen tenders to read, compare, clarify and assess before they can make a recommendation. They probably have to cope with a heavy workload anyway, and this means that most of the proposals they receive will be thrown away. There is a report which says that 75% of all tenders received by large organisations (e.g. large companies and government departments) are inadequate, in that they are discarded after just the first reading. Only 10% of the tenders received are considered for an award of a contract. That means that the effort expended on the 90% of tenders that have no chance of success is completely wasted by industry.

If your proposal is unclear, there will be doubt in your customer's mind after they have read it. They may not have understood what you were trying to explain. They may be confused. When it comes to assessment, they will add in contingencies, which will result in raising the price you have quoted.

These contingencies are to account for the risk that they might have to spend more to make your equipment or service fit their requirements. This is the best you can hope for. They may simply discard your proposal in favour of another, so you must always consider your customer.

Sub-contracting and teaming

Gone are the days when a single organisation could handle the majority of contracts by itself. This is partly because organisations have become more specialised and partly because purchasers have more comprehensive requirements – fewer, but larger, contracts. You will therefore be involved in sub-contracting part of the contract or working in collaboration with others. It is not uncommon to sub-contract 80% of a contract. You must therefore consider the best form of relationship with others. Will you sub-contract the work to them on a contract by contract basis? Or will you want to develop a longer-term relationship, spanning contracts over several years? Will you wish to form a partnership or joint venture? The answers will vary from contract to contract and from partner to partner.

Once you have decided how you will work with others in delivering the contract you then need to decide whom to involve in producing the proposal. In some cases, where the sub-contracted work is of a specialist nature, the answer will be obvious – use the expertise of the specialist. In other cases you may wish to confirm prices from major sub-contractors and use your estimating skills or an established factor for the minor sub-contracts. The more people involved, the more difficult it is to produce a coherent proposal, especially as there is never as much time as you would like.

Therefore you have to work out how to put the proposal together as a team, sort out the roles of the various parties, establish deadlines and agree on a common style. You also have to agree how to manage the production of the proposal.

Customer ethics

At the heart of the tendering process is the desire to preserve its integrity. Everyone is dealt with on an equal basis. The system should be fair – the 'level playing field' beloved by the European Commission. The competitive tendering process will not work unless everyone has faith in it. Most organisations in the public and private sectors abide by the ethical code of the Chartered Institute of Purchasing and Supply (CIPS), in spirit if not in overt recognition. The CBI and other organisations also publish codes of business ethics which contain almost identical provisions.

The Chartered Institute of Purchasing and Supply

The CIPS offers the following guidance in its ethical code:

- **Declaration of interest** – Any personal interest which may impinge on a purchasing officer's impartiality in any matter relevant to his or her duties should be declared.

- **Confidentiality and accuracy of information** – The confidentiality of information received in the course of duty should be respected and should never be used for personal gain; information given in the course of duty should be true and fair and never designed to mislead.

- **Competition** – While bearing in mind the advantages to the employing organisation of maintaining a continuing relationship with a supplier, any arrangement that might in the long-term prevent the effective operation of fair competition should be avoided.

- **Business gifts** – Other than items of very small intrinsic value such as business diaries or calendars, these should not be accepted.

- **Hospitality** – Modest hospitality is an accepted courtesy of a business relationship. However, the recipient should not allow him or herself to reach a position whereby he or she might be deemed by others to have been influenced in making a business decision as a consequence of accepting such hospitality; the frequency and scale of hospitality accepted should not be significantly greater than the recipient's employer would be likely to provide in return.

Very similar rules will apply to most customers' organisations in the majority of the countries of the world. However, every organisation is different and some have very strict rules concerning their dealings with suppliers, not allowing any gifts or hospitality of any kind. Always respect the rules imposed by your customers, otherwise the problems you create will count against you.

It is true that some customers do not follow these codes of ethics, but these are an exception. Tendering only works as a means of acquiring goods and services if all the parties involved believe that they are being treated fairly. Purchasers who abuse the principles soon acquire a reputation and then find it difficult to get suppliers to commit the time and effort to producing tenders. Remember that the aim is to end up with a successful contract. It will be much more difficult to achieve this working with an organisation that abuses the system.

By contrast, in a few countries standards are different. The payment of money to obtain introductions, appear on tender lists or to win the bidding is expected or demanded. In these cases be very careful and make sure you do your homework properly.

How European rules can help you

THE PUBLIC PROCUREMENT DIRECTIVES

NOTICES

SPECIFICATIONS

WHERE TO FIND INFORMATION

chapter 2

Chapter 2:
How European rules can help you

The European Commission is concerned about the competitiveness of Europe compared to other economic regions and decided some time ago that one problem was the lack of competition across national borders. It therefore commissioned a report by an Italian economist, Cecchini, which showed that only some 4% of public sector purchases came from outside the home state. Bearing in mind that this included the Benelux group of countries, the Commission determined to open up public sector procurement to more competition, in the hope that this would improve the competitiveness of the contractors and suppliers bidding for the work.

Public sector spending, that is spending by central and local government, accounts for the larger share of spend covered by the new European procurement rules. Although it is estimated by the Commission that more is spent on supplies than on works, because a works contract is inherently less mobile than supplies or services and therefore less open to cross-border trading, the threshold values above which the rules apply are much higher for works. Possibly because of the higher value and higher public profile of major construction projects the first area to be covered by legislation was works.

The public procurement directives

Rules governing the award of public works contracts were implemented as long ago as 1 January 1973 in Directive 71/305/EEC. They were, however, honoured more in the breach than in the observance. The provisions have been updated in Directives 78/669/EEC and 89/440/EEC, the latter applying from 19 July 1990. Most recently, Directive 93/37/EEC has been adopted by the Council of Ministers to consolidate the previous directives. The main provisions relating to works remain unchanged, however. In addition the public sector compliance Directive 89/665/EEC lays down the procedure for dealing with member states that fail to implement the rules.

Supplies were covered from 1977 in a number of different directives which were consolidated by Directive 93/36/EEC which came into force on 14 June 1994.

Services have been covered from 1 July 1993 under Directive 92/50/EEC.

Utility companies (those in water, electricity, gas, coal, oil, transport and telecommunications) have been covered since 1 January 1992 under Directive COM 90/531

which covered supplies and works. The Utilities Directive has been amended in 93/38/EEC to cover service contracts as well, with effect from mid 1994, and again in 98/4/EC to implement the provisions of the Government Procurement Agreement. Current proposals are to remove telecoms companies from coverage along with others which are now in competitive markets.

Implementation in the UK

The directives are implemented in the main via Statutory Instruments (SIs). Public sector supplies are covered by SI 1995/201 which replaced SI 1991/2679. Public sector works are implemented via SI 1991/2680 and public sector services are implemented by SI 1993/3228. These three SIs also cover compliance in the public sector.

Utilities are covered by SI 1996/2911, the Utilities Contracts Regulations 1996, which covers the procurement of supplies, works and services by utility organisations and also provides for associated remedies available to aggrieved contractors.

Notices

Every contract which falls above certain threshold values should be covered by three notices:

- The first is a Prior Information Notice (or Periodic Indicative Notice) (PIN). This is a general notice published by the purchaser indicating the contracts they intend to award over the following twelve months. This is the time to start making contact with the purchaser if you are not in regular contact already. Utilities can also use this notice as the call for competition, but should include the fuller information required for a Contract Notice.

- The second is a specific Contract Notice (or call for competition). This contains more details about a particular contract and must be published earlier than specified periods (roughly five weeks) before the tender list is chosen or tenders are due to be received. Utilities have the option of publishing a notice about a vendor qualification system instead and using that as the call for competition. In all cases you need to be aware of the time taken to process applications, since this can be considerable.

- The third is the Contract Award Notice (CAN), which the purchaser publishes once the contract has been awarded. This is designed to give tenderers an idea of the contracts being awarded by a particular purchaser. In particular, for contracts for services, the CAN should cover certain services which are not advertised in advance (such as legal services).

It is a fact that purchasers are still poor at publishing PINs and CANs, and for those contracts that are advertised often only the Contract Notice appears. It is also a fact that if the first you hear about a particular contract requirement is via a Contract Notice it is usually too late to be considered seriously. This does not mean you should not respond to the notice – most contracts are repeated at regular intervals and responding to one notice may put you in line to be a serious contender for following contracts. You must also remember that many contracts are not advertised at all. Therefore, it is vital to make contact with prospective customers in advance to find out if any potential contracts are coming up.

Specifications

The purchaser's specification should have been written to incorporate European specifications where these exist. Where they do not, the purchaser's requirements must be defined as far as possible by reference to other standards in use in Europe, whether these are international or national standards or other standards adopted by a recognised standards-making body.

Any requirements which cannot be specified by the above standards should be defined by reference to performance requirements rather than specific design or description characteristics. In particular, specific makes should not be referred to unless this is completely unavoidable, when the words 'or equivalent' must be used.

Any supplier or contractor is entitled to ask for a copy of a purchaser's specification, although the purchaser may choose to impose a charge, to prevent frivolous enquiries. Such a charge, however, must be imposed on all, and if set too high, will discourage genuine tenderers. It is supposed to cover only copying, postage and administration costs.

The specification should also include the criteria that will be used to assess the tenders, normally in descending order of importance, unless these have been included in the notice calling for tenders or expressions of interest.

Where to find information

Information about opportunities to tender in Europe is contained in notices which are published in the Supplement to the *Official Journal of the European Communities* (OJEC 'S' series). This appears daily but is no longer published on paper. Instead you can subscribe to a daily or twice-weekly CD-ROM which contains all the notices in the various languages in Europe. You should be aware that full information will only normally appear in the language of the purchaser. Alternatively you can get hold of the notices published each day, free of charge, on the Internet. One good route is via the European Commission's own procurement website: http://simap.eu.int/

European public purchasers are increasingly being encouraged to provide links to their own websites in notices and to put full information about the opportunities available on those sites.

Many organisations will seek help from others. Many trade associations scan the *Official Journal* and other publications for notices of relevance to their members. Chambers of commerce may do the same. There are also a series of Euro Info Centres around the country who will help bidders seek the information they need.

In addition to the official information sources there are several private sector newspapers and information sources which bidders can subscribe to. *Contrax Weekly* is one such publication. As well as categorising the information in ways which the publishers believe are more helpful to bidders, they usually contain information about other contracts which are not published at European level, either because they fall below the relevant threshold values, or because they are exempt for other reasons.

Finally, don't forget to read the trade press for your industry. Newspapers and magazines often publish information about forthcoming contracts, either in lists or in articles about new projects.

The bidding decision

chapter

Chapter 3:
The bidding decision

Probably the single most important decision to be made in the tendering process is whether to bid or not to bid. It is inevitable that you will not win every tender, and a considerable amount of the effort which goes into preparing tenders and proposals is therefore wasted. The most successful companies decide what their strategy is, adopt a plan to follow it and think very carefully before deciding whether to bid or not. Concentrating on producing a few good tenders will always result in an increased amount of successful business than chasing every opportunity offered. You need to concentrate your efforts and resources on those areas which are likely to offer the best returns – both in chances of winning the tendering and in obtaining profitable work.

Early tracking of prospects

It is vitally important to be aware of the opportunities coming up as early as possible. Not only does this give you the best chance to prepare for the tender, but it also gives you the greatest opportunity to influence the format and content to your advantage. Purchasers are busy people and also recognise they are not the experts in every subject. If you offer advice and assistance at an early stage this will often be welcomed. The same advice and assistance offered just before the tenders are due in will be viewed with great suspicion. The best time to become involved is before the proposals have been put in writing. They are much easier to change at this stage. Once written proposals start circulating within the customer's organisation they are harder to change, and much harder still once they have been published to the outside world.

Why do you want to get involved early? The main reason is to ensure you have an opportunity to put forward your good ideas. Tendering is a formal process and purchasers tend to take a conservative approach during tendering. To do otherwise would be to give an apparent advantage to one or other bidder. You therefore find you are responding to a specification put forward by the purchaser. If your response does not match that specification, the purchaser is likely to put your tender to one side, especially if they have compliant bids from others. Think for a minute how you win business. You do so by being better than the competition in one or more respects. This is your competitive advantage. You need to make sure that your customers value your special qualities, not just in their minds, but

23

in their specifications and assessment processes. Make sure that whatever is unique to you is marked, preferably with a high weighting. This is why you need to become involved with the customer at an early stage of the process. Obviously this is much easier with an existing customer with whom you have current work, but you should also be making contact with prospective customers with whom you really want to do business.

Bidder conferences

Some purchasers organise bidder conferences to explain any peculiarities of the project under consideration and to ensure that all bidders receive the same information. Other purchasers prefer to keep their bidders apart, hoping they will not know who the competition is. If there are special circumstances surrounding the tender and it is not clear from the published documents what is required, you should always request clarification from the customer. If the customer is concerned about treating all bidders equally you may wish to suggest they hold a bidders' conference. This will save much potentially wasted effort, because the usual result of unclear requirements is a re-issued enquiry.

If a conference is held, you must make sure you attend. Otherwise you may miss vital information, which you will probably be deemed to have had anyway. Attending the conference will also allow you to confirm who is competing against you and will give you a better idea of the solution anticipated by the purchaser. The conference may be your only opportunity to clarify what the purchaser's real requirements and priorities are at this stage, but any answers given are available to everyone present. If you have a novel solution to suggest which will improve your competitive position you may not want to air this in public. If so, you may have to test your ideas on the purchaser before the formal tender is issued, which is why it is so important to get involved at the earliest stage possible.

Analysis of the requirements

Once the purchaser's documents have been received (or they may have been communicated by telephone, fax, and e-mail or in a meeting) you need to analyse how you can best meet their needs. You will need to work out whether you can meet these needs under a contract, which you can not only win, but which will also be profitable to your organisation. You should also be clear how winning the bidding will fit into your company strategy and planning. Will it help your organisation meet the goals that have been set?

You therefore need to work out an outline solution together with an outline cost as early as possible. Ask yourself: Will this solution meet the customer's requirements? Will the cost enable us to put in a price which will win the contract and still leave room for profit? Will the solution enable our organisation to make a significant contribution to the added value for the customer or will we have to sub-contract most of the significant work? If the answers to all these questions are positive for your organisation you need to consider how much effort and resources will be required to produce your tender. Can you meet the tender return deadline? Is the resource required commensurate with the likely future benefit?

Once you have the answers to these questions you will be in a position to make a very important decision, one which needs to be taken as early as possible.

Deciding whether or not to submit a bid

The decision whether to bid for a particular requirement or not is one of the most important decisions your organisation can ever take. Those companies who bid for everything that comes their way are not usually the most successful. Resources are scarce and there is always a conflict between putting your best people into winning new business or making sure existing contracts are as successful as possible. After all, the best way to win new business is to ensure that your existing business is performed well. It is always easier to retain an existing customer than to win a new one. So there is a dilemma, especially if there are problems on existing contracts. Resolving these to everyone's satisfaction may well lead to more profitable business in the future from that customer rather than devoting the same scarce resources to putting a bid into a new customer.

You must therefore consider very carefully which bids to submit and which to decline. This will allow you to concentrate your resources on those bids which stand the best chance of giving you a successful contract. If you have prepared your ground early enough you will have made it clear to prospective customers that you will be a good organisation to invite to tender for a particular requirement, or that the requirement does not really fit your organisation's expertise. This means that you will receive fewer formal enquiry documents, but those you do see should be of more interest to you.

However, often you do not know enough about the customer's prospective requirements until you see the enquiry documents. This is particularly likely if you are responding to open tender invitations advertised in the *European Official Journal* or in newspapers.

Whatever the decision, there are some rules you should always follow:

1. Make the decision whether to bid or not as early in the process as possible. Until the decision is made, you will be expending time and effort on the enquiry and if you decide not to proceed this will be wasted. Conversely, the time to submit a tender is always more limited than you would like and you need to start work as early as possible if the decision to proceed is made. Do not do as some organisations do – prepare the tender and then decide whether to submit it when it goes before a director at the last minute!

2. If you decide not to bid, inform the customer, again as early as possible. This is especially important if you one of a limited number of organisations invited to bid. It is also important if one of your salespeople has promised the customer that you are really interested in winning this contract. This may upset the customer a bit, but much less than simply not receiving a tender. If you decline early enough, the customer has a chance to find someone else. They may be required by their rules to find a certain minimum number of bidders. If, in response, the customer begs you to reconsider your decision, this could be an indication that they are really hoping that you will submit the winning tender. This may indicate that your chances of winning are higher than you thought, which may lead you to reconsider your decision. In that case, consider the next point.

3. If you need more time to prepare your bid, perhaps because key people will only become available later on in the process, ask for an extension of the tender response deadline. The customer's reply may give you a clue whether to proceed with a bid or not. If they flatly refuse, they may just not be interested in your tender, having someone else in mind. In that case, you have received a heavy hint as to what your decision should be, and you should save yourself further wasted effort. If, on the other hand, they are very accommodating, you may be able to take this as a good incentive to proceed with the bid.

4. If you decide to bid in principle, fix a budget for the bid. This may just consist of individuals' time, or it may need money as well. You need a certain minimum amount of resource to study the requirement – consider how you are going to meet the customer's needs, find the appropriate sub-contractors and partners and put the tender together. If this resource is not there, you will not be able to submit a good bid, and could possibly jeopardise your chances elsewhere by leaving another tender under-resourced.

5. Fix a timetable for producing the tender. Make sure this allows sufficient time for reviews by directors or senior managers before the bid is submitted. Sufficient time means that you can incorporate their comments into the final submitted tender. There is no point in receiving comments which are too late to incorporate. Also, make sure there is sufficient time in your timetable for physically producing the required number of copies and getting them to the customer.

As I mentioned above there are many good reasons to submit a tender. This will lead, if successful, to good business. Tendering is the source of much, if not most, of the work your organisation does. If you tender for nothing, you will not obtain the contracts you need to prosper and grow. However, this does not mean you should tender every opportunity that arises. The following are among the considerations when deciding whether to go for a particular opportunity:

- What are the chances of winning?
- How competitive is your organisation?
- What are your strengths?
- What are your weaknesses?
- What relationship do you have with the customer?
- How profitable will the resulting contract be?
- What are the risks?
- Do you have the capacity to carry out the contract?
- Does the contract help the long-term objectives of your organisation?

Let's consider each of these in turn.

What are the chances of winning?

Your chances of winning depend partly on the competition for a contract. If you are one of three bidding for a contract, all other factors being equal, you have a one in three chance of being successful. If you are one of 20 you only have a 5% chance of being successful. Therefore the potential reward from the contract in the latter case must be that much greater to compensate for the additional effort that will go towards unsuccessful tenders. If you have the choice, concentrate on tenders where the number of competitors is limited. Tendering is expensive and purchasers need to understand that they may not get a good response if they ask too many bidders to tender.

If you are responding to open tendering, where there is no pre-selection of bidders, you will not know how many tenders will be submitted, so you will not know what your chances are. You may not have a choice, if all opportunities in your area

of business are handled in this way, but many companies will not respond to open tender advertisements simply because the chances of winning are unknown. On the other hand, if you are working in a very specialised field, with only a limited number of competitors, open tendering will make little, if no, difference.

How competitive is your organisation?

You need to understand how competitive your organisation is. You can discover this through an analysis of your track record in tendering and through customer feedback. The more competitive you are the more likely you are to win the contract. However, the resulting contract may not be as profitable because of the competitive price. You clearly need to weigh up the volume of business you win against the profitability of the contracts you undertake. It is an individual decision whether to go for volume or high profitability and either approach has led to success for many companies.

If you are not competitive on price but offer other advantages (better performance, for example) then you must consider whether the customer will be willing to pay extra for the benefits you offer. Some customers are very price focused, and in these cases you would be better devoting your energy elsewhere and concentrating on those tenders where the customer appreciates the long-term benefits of your solution.

What are your strengths and weaknesses?

Every company has strengths and weaknesses. Be realistic about what these are for your organisation and consider whether the tender can take advantage of your strengths. If so, go for the opportunity, but if the customer appears to be focused on areas in which you are weak then you should be more inclined to decline to bid.

What relationship do you have with the customer?

Tenders are rarely submitted in isolation to a completely new customer. More often than not, they are part of a series of relationships between companies and this relationship helps determine your response to the enquiry. If the contracts you have won in the past have been considered a success by both parties then it must be worth trying for more contracts. If you know that your customer is very keen to see a tender from you, for whatever reason, then be predisposed to submit a tender, as much as anything to maintain good relations with that customer. If, however, current contracts are causing difficulties you need to address these difficulties before seeking further work from the customer.

How profitable will the resulting contract be?

When deciding whether to submit a tender consider how profitable the resulting contract is likely to be. If the potential rewards are great it will be more worthwhile to spend a larger amount on submitting a tender. Conversely, if the rewards will be small there is less benefit in working on the tender in the first place.

What are the risks?

You should also consider the risks associated both with the tendering process and with any resulting contract. Obviously, the riskier the contract, the higher the profitability you should be seeking in compensation. A risky, low-margin contract will not be worth tendering unless you have other strategic reasons for so doing. However, there may also be risks in submitting or failing to submit a tender. Some purchasers require you to give a bid bond, which you may forfeit if you do not accept a contract that is offered to you. Therefore you should check that you have the capacity to deliver the contract if required. You may also need to clarify the likely conditions of contract at an early stage. You may have a particular relationship with a customer which leads them to expect a tender from you every time. Failure to submit a tender in these circumstances may jeopardise you receiving enquiries in the future, and if they are an important customer it will be less risky to submit a tender, even if you think the likelihood of winning the business is remote.

Do you have the capacity to carry out the contract?

One major risk concerns your capacity to carry out the contract if you win. At any one time you may be tendering for three times as much work as you can carry out. You must consider what you will do if every tender is successful. But your decision on whether to submit a bid is also based on the capacity available to you. If you have spare capacity you must pursue new business vigorously, whereas if your capacity is stretched you may find it beneficial to devote your resources to completing existing contracts instead.

More immediately, you must determine whether you have the resources to prepare the tender. If not, your decision is made for you.

Does the contract help the long-term objectives of your organisation?

You should consider the long-term objectives of your organisation. Are you seeking to increase your business in a particular market or are you aiming to withdraw from that market? The tenders you submit should reflect your strategic and other plans.

29

All these factors will influence your decision, but once you take that decision, stick to it. If you decide to submit a tender, do it properly with enough resources to produce a good tender within the required timescale.

Prequalification

THE CUSTOMER'S PROCESS FOR SELECTING BIDDERS

THE PRINCIPAL OBJECTIVES

chapter **4**

Chapter 4:
Prequalification

Some people regard prequalification as a completely separate process from tendering, but in fact most tendering in the West involves some form of prequalification. Prequalification is the first stage in the process and it is necessary to pass this in order to get onto a tender list.

The customer's process for selecting bidders

Different customers have different approaches to tendering but most involve reducing the number of potential tenderers down to a manageable size. The more professional customers will be trying to ensure the best tenderers are those left on the final short list. As far as the customer is concerned the best tenderers are the ones who are best suited technically to deliver a solution to the customer and who are also keenest to win the work. This will deliver the customer a technically suitable solution at the best price. The customer will therefore be looking for information to help them choose:

- Those companies who fit comfortably with their way of working

- Those companies who have had experience of doing similar work before

- Those companies who are most competitive at the size of contract being contemplated

- Those companies who are very keen to work with the customer.

Typically the customer starts by issuing a questionnaire to potential tenderers seeking information about the tenderers' finances, staff, organisation, assets, quality assurance procedures, health and safety record, environmental and ethical policies and previous contracts undertaken. This may be specific to the contract in question, or may be issued as part of a vendor qualification system, in which case the information will be used for many contracts. Some customers use third-party systems run on their behalf by others. These third-party systems usually cover several customers, so more effort may be justified in supplying them with information.

Although half the potential tenderers drop out at this stage, because they do not complete or return the questionnaire, the customer may still feel that they have too many to shortlist. They may therefore seek additional information relevant to the contract, especially if they have collected general information for a standing

qualification system. This may be through a further questionnaire, or they may summon vendors to an interview or visit them.

It is at this stage that tenderers become qualified for consideration for the tender list, with pre-qualification being awarded to those who successfully complete the first questionnaire. However, particularly with third party systems, there may be little or no element of judgement following the first questionnaire stage. In this case the system should be regarded as one of registration, rather than qualification. In any case, these stages need to be completed successfully to allow you to remain on the short list.

The principal objectives

Your objective is to stay under consideration throughout the process and not to give the purchaser reasons to eliminate you from further consideration. To do this you must:

- Return the documents or supply the information requested promptly and certainly within the stated time limits. If you need more time, ask for this. Simply ignoring a stated return date and supplying late information may mean that all your efforts are wasted.

- Supply complete information. Answer all the questions you can. However, carefully consider whether to answer questions seeking commercially confidential information. Think how much information your competitors are likely to supply but also consider how badly you want the contract.

- Supply truthful information. For public sector and utility purchasers one of the few reasons allowed for outright rejection is serious misrepresentation. Even if not discovered at the time and you win the contract, such misrepresentation can justify the purchaser in instant termination of the contract during its progress, so do not tell lies. Clearly it would be sensible to put your organisation in the best possible light, so you can select your best contracts as your chosen references.

- Supply relevant information. If you have to choose which information to supply select that which relates to previous contracts with the purchaser, or failing that, previous contracts in the relevant sector and/or geographical area. Purchasers will be much more impressed by experience which relates to their circumstances.

- Follow clues given by the purchaser. If you are asked about a health and safety policy, an environmental policy, or an ethical policy, this means

that the purchaser expects you to have one. The questions asked may even tell you what that policy should be. Use these to develop one if you do not have one in place already.

The purchaser is trying to find the best bidders. This means that they will often mark the questionnaires returned to them. As well as needing to remain under consideration you also want to score as high a mark as possible at each stage. This is done by providing relevant and complete information. Sometimes these assessment scores are carried forward to the main tender assessment, so answer the questions as best as you can. This does also mean you may not score well where you are not well suited to the prospective contract. Recognise this as a fact as early as possible and cut your losses by withdrawing, so that you can concentrate your resources on those tenders where you do stand a good chance.

Planning and organising for the tender

TEAM ORGANISATION AND PLANNING

ESTIMATING AND SUB-CONTRACTORS

TENDER SETTLING

IDEAS, OPTIONS AND SOLUTIONS

chapter **5**

Chapter 5:
Planning and organising for the tender

You are often not alone but are part of a team of individuals who need to produce the tender. Even if you work alone on this task you will almost certainly need information from sub-contractors and suppliers to include in your document.

The production of a proposal should be treated as a mini project. Apply classical project management techniques to it. Each project is unique, so is each proposal.

Define the objectives, write them down and circulate them. Make sure they are realistic! Proposals are often done in quite short time scales and it is important that each step is given a sensible proportion of this short time.

Produce plans which are clear and effective, ones that are credible and workable – ones that fit the size and scope of the proposal. Clearly structure the proposal and its production.

Remember to allow time for a review of your tender and programme this so that there is still time to change things if necessary.

Team organisation and planning

Divide the task into component parts and assign responsibilities to each. Create work packages. If the task is large, then create a work breakdown structure. If the customer has done this for you in their request for proposal, then your initial task is easier – follow what your customer has done.

Measure progress and create sensible means of control. Make sure it is understood and is responsive. Hold reviews, expedite problems, and monitor costs and the price build-up.

Make the leadership effective. Create clear rules and get people involved. Make sure the lines of communication are clear and open throughout the bid preparation team. Call a kick-off meeting for everyone likely to be involved, explain the background, the strategy and the tactics.

Make teamwork happen through appropriate leadership, consistent rules and a 'team first' culture. Co-ordinate technical and commercial matters, expedite problems, encourage and cajole. Co-ordinate all the efforts.

The strategy for the tender

A number of topics have to be looked at here and they have to be sorted in the light of what is important to the customer and you. Typically you should consider the following. Add or delete as necessary, but do define a strategy.

Aim to meet the submission dates. Often a late submission will be rejected out of hand. Your customer has a strict timetable to meet and if you create delay, then you will be marked down. If you can't deliver a tender on time, what chances have you of delivering the project on time?

Determine the customer's decision making and assessment criteria. Have you got them? How can you get them? Can you make an intelligent guess at them? What is the customer's attitude to various subcontractors?

What are the strengths of the company and what is the best way of playing them? Which ones will score most heavily over the competition?

What are your weaknesses, how should you field them to minimise the adverse effects on your bid? How should you exploit the weaknesses of the competition? Play up their vulnerabilities and mask their strengths.

Identify and manage risky areas. Maybe these are difficult performance targets, maybe the risk is too one sided (biased against you of course). Can you offer a relaxation on targets for a better price? Put in contingencies as appropriate, but make sure this process is well managed. It is not a recipe for a winning price when everybody who contributes to the tender puts in their own contingency without reference to anybody else.

Planning the tender

The plans you make must reflect how you do business and the culture of your company. Consider the size of the bid, is it small or large? What is the timescale to prepare it? Is the customer a new one or an old friend? What is the forward workload of the factory? All these affect the way the tender is planned so the notes here are only a guide and should be interpreted accordingly.

Define a 'win' strategy and central theme to form the basis of internal guidance to contributors. Try to achieve a balance between technical and management themes. Produce a score sheet which reflects the customer's assessment criteria (this is discussed below). Plan the resources, prepare the directives and schedule the reviews. You have to convince management of the cost of winning, because they have to release the funds for the tender preparation process.

The actual work plan can range from a simple list of dates for the critical targets, through a time planner which details the activities and their planned and actual completion dates, to a fully fledged bar chart showing all the interrelated activities. It depends on the size and scope of the job as to which level is selected as appropriate.

Directives

Directives are instruction sheets for each contributor (including yourself) for each section. They assign responsibility and provide guidelines. They set out the themes and strategies, what to work in and what to skate around. They can also contain checklists for compliance and publication standards and budgets for larger tenders.

Directives should be looked on as a means of leaving nothing to chance, or to personal interpretation of others in the organisation.

Compliance matrix

A compliance matrix can be an extremely useful tool in checking that your tender covers every aspect of the purchaser's enquiry. One side lists all the requirements of the purchaser against page or paragraph numbers in the enquiry, while the other shows the page number, section or paragraph number in your tender which deals with that point. Not only does this clearly show which sections of your tender remain to be completed, but it can also help the customer find their way through your tender.

Consider including your compliance matrix in the tender you submit. If the customer can clearly see where their requirements are answered this will make their life easier. This is particularly important for complicated tenders, especially where your tender does not follow the same order as the customer's enquiry.

Score sheets

A score sheet is constructed early in the programme and completed during various reviews. The squares can be marked or scored. Either way, it is a visual method of seeing at a glance where your weaknesses are in the tender. Early identification of these is essential if you want to correct them.

The aim is to get as close as possible to the customer's assessment methods and criteria.

Pricing methodology

It is necessary to update your anticipated costs and prices to try to make them compatible. Marketing should be trying to establish a price for the job and from this you can start to allocate target costs to all areas.

You are aiming to establish a baseline for the design and then to compare the design to the cost targets. It is often necessary to make a number of iterations to reduce any problems to (hopefully) zero. You may already do this informally but with a large and complex tender, it needs to be done in a controlled and formal way.

Estimating and sub-contractors

Tender periods are always shorter than the ideal and therefore the manager of the tendering team must get as many activities working in parallel as possible. Items that need early attention include:

- Legal review of the proposed contract terms and identification of any aspects which need to be qualified in the tender. If the purchaser has either written their own terms or heavily modified a standard form then this activity can be very time consuming.

- Parent company guarantees and/or performance bonds, which may be required, pose particular administrative difficulties for subsidiaries of large organisations, especially where the ultimate holding company is based outside the UK.

- Investigation of the financial soundness of the purchaser.

- Sub-contracts may form a significant part of the works and so these need to be managed with care. These enquiries are small versions of the main enquiry, deserving the same attention. They should include: instructions to tenderers, description of the scope of work, technical specification, commercial specification detailing the proposed form of subcontract, main contract, payment terms and project management requirements.

- If in-house design is required this needs to be started as soon as possible.

- There are a number of techniques which may be used to estimate costs and these are discussed in Chapter 6 (page 46).

- A comprehensive technical proposal may well be required and, although it may be possible to base this on earlier offers, it needs to be tailored for the current enquiry. A careful purchaser will include in their enquiry sufficient tender schedules to ensure that they understand the important details of the offer. However, if these are not supplied then the tender

team must compile their own documentation clearly defining what is being offered.

- Similarly a commercial proposal is required and it may also be necessary to demonstrate that the project will be managed effectively.

The overall cost build-up and subsequent pricing takes place late in the tender period once the subcontractors' offers have been received.

Tender settling

Large organisations that have to submit complex tenders nearly always split the production of the bid into separate teams and these are most commonly designated by colours. When it comes to reviewing the tender, the Blue Team is made up from the tender team itself, with members reviewing the sections produced by each other. The Red Team is an objective third party review. It can come from colleagues within the organisation who have had nothing to do with the tender production to date, or it can be made up of outsiders. The financial elements of the tender may be reviewed separately by a Gold Team (also known as the Yellow Team) while the final sign-off by senior management is often called the Black Hat review. The most important of these reviews is the Red Team.

The mention of a Red Team should not dissuade those writing small tenders from taking this philosophy on board. The word 'team' originated from those writing substantial proposals where you did in fact have teams of people doing reviewing jobs. For small tenders, it can be a Red Person.

The Red Team simulates the customer. They start by reading the customer's request for tender and then judge how well the written tender communicates its content to 'the customer'. Ideally the Red Team should have no contact with the tender writers until review time, but in small organisations this may be impossible to achieve.

The Red Team uses the score sheet (prepared earlier) to evaluate the final drafts, hopefully the same score sheet that the customer will use. Comments from the Red Team are pinned to the wall beneath the final drafts of the modules. If necessary they can discuss with the authors any problems which crop up and maybe they can help with the rewrites when time is running short or the author is wide of the mark.

The score sheet should highlight major deficiencies, although there ought not to be any of these at this late stage. The score sheet should also help to achieve a balance across the tender ensuring that proper emphasis is placed at the crucial points in the tender.

The Red Team must not attempt any redesign. They must not look at the tender from their own viewpoint; it should be looked at from the customer's viewpoint. They must not interact with the tender team during the evaluation nor should they depart from the procedures. Trying to wear two quite different hats at the same time dilutes the crucial part they have to play.

Ideas, options and solutions

Innovation is the key factor in company success. Innovation can be born of necessity but it is best derived from a managed process of development. The significance that innovations have in the tendering process is quite often overlooked.

When a job has been won, the job is designed, made and delivered exactly as described in the tender. Similarly, any service must be provided as described in the proposal. Any new ideas, novelties, etc., which arise are carefully stored away to be incorporated in the next round of bidding. Ideas get fed into tenders and become part of the product line of the company.

Ideas arrive from within your company and from outside. However it must not be forgotten that the culture of the company must be receptive to new ideas, they must have the support of the top executive. Perhaps the corporate plan has a phrase in it which seeks to promote creativity and the exploitation of new ideas.

New ideas for tenders are of necessity the result of short-term needs. Generally just looking at the service or product required will suggest improvements that can be introduced in the time available. Creativity in all its forms can generally be used in tenders. Mind mapping, brainstorming, synectics and lateral thinking all have their place and have been used to good effect at times.

However, it is important that you examine whether the customer will be responsive to new ideas or alternative solutions first. Does the customer's specification allow alternative technical solutions? Have they made up their mind? Will they be amenable to a variety of ideas? Naturally, if the answer is 'No' to all these, then you are wasting your time producing a lot of options for the customer to choose from.

However, if the customer is amenable to change, then you have to ascertain how they will make up their mind, how they will choose, what criteria they will use, and what happens if these criteria tend to change.

41

Assessment of options

The simplest method of selecting the appropriate option is intuitive, often referred to as a 'wet finger in the air'. This is not always the best way to go forward, you have no control over the process and often nobody can be made to be responsible for the decision.

A better way and one which is quite often used is a direct comparison of figures. They may be cost or a measure of performance. You can compare cars by looking at their top speeds or their consumption figures. This method is fine if the number of criteria is very small – one or two.

When the number of criteria approaches half a dozen, then resorting to a graphical comparison is often the easiest way around the problem. The performance polygon is a sensible method in these circumstances, but it does have the drawback that the axes can be tailored to reach a preferred (biased) solution.

Finally, when the number of criteria are very large, only a numerical analysis will achieve results. This process sometimes goes under the name of 'Trade Studies' or 'Trade off Studies'. Here numbers are allocated to certain characteristics and each alternative is assessed as to how well they conform to each characteristic. If they conform 100% they are given a high mark, say 10, and they are given lower marks as their conformance diminishes. Each of the characteristics are weighted, that is given another score to show how important that particular characteristic is. The weight can be 10 for very important to 1 for being of minor importance. The individual marks are multiplied by the weightings for those particular characteristics and these weighted marks are finally totalled to give the 'overall score' for that option. The option with the highest score wins.

If, during a tender preparation phase, you want to perform a trade study on some options, you need to get the weightings that your customer will be using. If these are unavailable, then you will have to make an informed guess as to what they will be using.

In order to give yourself the best possible opportunity to introduce your ideas you should speak to the customer as early as possible, before any formal enquiry documents are issued. Customers are most likely to consider alternatives when they still have to write the specification. Speaking to them early means that you can ensure that your ideas will be considered by the customer when you submit your tender.

Pricing and risk management

chapter **6**

Chapter 6:
Pricing and risk management

Before the price is fixed for any contract it is important to know what your costs are for the work. Most organisations use cost related systems to arrive at their selling price, either by adding a fixed percentage to their costs or taking a fixed margin off their selling price.

Defining what has to be costed

As far as the purchaser is concerned the seller's price is a cost. To this, the purchaser has to add their associated costs. If the purchaser is at the end of the chain – if they are the ultimate customer – these associated costs may include:

• *design*	• *storage*	• *running costs*
• *consultancy*	• *installation*	• *maintenance*
• *inspection*	• *testing*	• *spare parts*
• *insurance*	• *commissioning*	• *repairs*
• *transport*	• *finance*	• *legal costs*

This list is not exhaustive. There may be questions of staffing, decommissioning, etc.

On the other hand if the purchaser themselves is in the middle of the chain, then in their role as supplier we can write:

cost = labour + materials + subcontracts + expenses + overheads

price = cost + profit

In this equation, the seller's 'price' appears as an element of *materials* or *subcontracts*. These are sometimes known as the merchant account.

As well as the cost or 'base estimate' (BE) for the total scope of responsibilities detailed in the enquiry or invitation to tender or bid (ITT/ITB) from the customer, there needs to be added a risk provision for any contract of any complexity.

This is arrived at from an experienced assessment and analysis of all the risks inherent in the contract under the terms of contract being proposed by the client. It is not normally possible to include the total financial consequences of all poten-

tial risks as this would lead to a non-competitive cost estimate. The question of probability therefore has to be introduced. It is important to recognise that risk provision is an element of the cost estimate and not a 'margin'. The assessment must not therefore be affected by the competitive market situation.

The profit is arrived at by a commercial decision related to the likely level of competition. If you consider it necessary to subsidise the price in order to secure the contract, the profit will be negative at the point of sale.

Direct costs

The direct costs or base estimate will probably constitute over 90% of the price, so it is vital to establish it at a high confidence level. This can only be achieved by authorising the expenditure of sufficient man-hours to produce a high quality proposal. Direct costs will be made up of costs in three main categories. The standard format used by one major company is shown in Appendix 1 (page 117) and lists the components of the three categories.

In-house recoveries

This category will typically constitute about 15-30% of the base estimate and must be estimated in detail with care. It includes all the man-hours estimated on a discipline by discipline basis to execute the contract. To achieve an acceptable estimate the head of each discipline must approve the man-hour estimate for that discipline and take responsibility for it during contract execution. In the case of item 1.2 – Engineering in the example (see Appendix 1 page 117), each sub-discipline will establish its own estimate, e.g. civil, structural, mechanical, electrical, instrumentation, pipework and process. In-house costs should be established by multiplying the man-hour estimates by standard costing rates. In many companies these will include direct overhead costs (as in the example) hence item 1.10 is used to add the indirect overhead element.

Merchant account

This category, which includes everything purchased outside your organisation, will typically constitute 50-65% or more of the base estimate hence it is crucial to have a high confidence level in this element. Maximum support must be obtained from vendors and subcontractors. This support will only be reliable if the prices submitted have been based on detailed specifications, a clear definition of responsibilities and scope and similar contract conditions to those in the client's ITT. The validity of support prices must be such as to carry through to the point when

it would be possible to place an order after securing the contract from the client. Such validities therefore may need regular extension as negotiations proceed.

Where delivery obligations are included you should obtain prices from reputable shipping and forwarding agents and where overseas shipment is required such prices must be based on the appropriate INCOTERMS. In-house estimating should be limited to items being manufactured in-house or being purchased from standard price lists. You should maintain an in-house up-to-date database as a check on both vendors' prices and in-house estimates. Continuous refining of prices from vendors and subcontractors should continue right up to the finalising of the base estimate and the commencement of the risk analysis.

Estimating and sub-contractors

The above covers large capital projects. In other circumstances there are a number of techniques which you may use to estimate costs:

- **Global estimating** – This uses general historical data to provide some indication of the likely costs, e.g. the cost per megawatt installed of diesel generator plant.

- **Factorial estimating** – Prices are sought from sub-contractors for the main items of plant but peripheral items are priced using historical data. This technique is often used in process plants.

- **Man-hour estimating** – This is useful where there is a significant labour content, e.g. engineering design and drawing production.

- **Unit rate estimating** – This is often used in building work where the rates for different activities, e.g. plastering, are well defined.

- **Operational estimating** – This is the most comprehensive form of estimating where the work is planned in detail and costed at current rates. If possible, firm quotations, valid for at least the validity of the main offer, are obtained for all the main items.

The overall cost build-up and subsequent pricing takes place late in the tender period once you have received the subcontractors' offers.

Other costs

This category will typically constitute 10% to 15% of the base estimate. These costs include royalties and licences, agents' commissions, taxes and duties, finance for cash flow, insurances, bonds and guarantees, project financing (if applicable) and credit insurance. These are all items where accurate cost estimates can be established.

Risk provision

One relatively simple method is put forward here. It has proved reliable over a period of several years and has succeeded in eliminating a high proportion of the profit erosion which used to take place in one major international contractor, from the point of sale to the completion of the contract. Furthermore, it has in many cases led to profit enhancement. The aim of the method is to identify all potential risks, then to respond to them by rejection or amelioration. Where possible through discussions with the customer, transfer risk to vendors, subcontractors and insurance companies and arrive at a list of accepted risks.

It is then necessary to address this list in order to assess the potential risk and/or benefit for each item on a financial basis. A major policy decision is then required as to what probability percentage the company's Board will accept for breaking even on the base estimate plus the Risk Provision (i.e. the total cost estimate). Let us assume this is 85%, then a simple calculation will allow you to arrive at a corrected Risk Provision 'R' which must be added to the Base Estimate (BE) to give the Cost Estimate. In some companies the approach is based on the following concepts:

- All risk analysis in most types of business is subjective and based on the collective experience of those carrying it out and the database of the company's past successes/failures.

- It must be standardised such that a common thought process is brought to bear by all participants.

- It must be simple and quick to operate.

- It is expected that the maximum experience will be assembled to carry it out at one session and the maximum number of relevant elemental factors will be examined.

- The group will set a level of probability with which it is comfortable and which will be applied by all operating companies in all risk analyses.

- The process must not be affected by any consideration of what the market will stand. Market forces affect the profit level, not the risk provision which must be considered to be part of the cost.

The method used is as follows. Five major categories of risk are examined, namely:

1. Estimating accuracy

This is divided into sub-categories such as merchant account costs, man-hours, in-house manufacture, shipping and transport, expense items and so on, comprising all elements of the estimate. Merchant account costs (i.e. external purchases) and man-hours are broken down into the various disciplines involved.

2. Degree of definition

The impact of the degree of definition of the ITT and in the proposal is assessed on various elements of the cost estimate, e.g. engineering, procurement construction, and plant performance tests.

3. Contract conditions

The various liabilities and risks in the commercial contract are assessed. This is a very important part of the analysis and will include such items as client involvement, late/early completion penalty/bonus, prolongation costs, rectification/make good costs, plant performance penalties, defects liabilities and so on.

4. Financial risks

This section will include non-payment risk, cash flow finance, calling of bonds and guarantees, duties and taxes and other such risks.

5. Sitework risks

These may be assessed in the above sections, but include civil works growth, design errors, soil conditions, climate and seismological conditions, acceleration costs, etc.

The technique is to take the appropriate elemental cost and assess a percentage potential risk and benefit and translate these into absolute risk and benefit. The summation of all the risks and benefits gives the total potential risk and benefit, namely the Rt and Bt. If the cost estimate was established, considering only risks and ignoring the benefits you would have:

Cost = Base Estimate (BE) + Rt

but you would probably price yourselves out of the market so you have to apply an acceptable probability factor P and determine by how much you can reduce Rt. The formulae used are:

$Rc = Rt - \triangle R$

where Rc is the corrected risk provision and:

$$\triangle R = \sqrt{\frac{(100 - P)}{100}\ (Rt + Bt)(Rt)}$$

This is derived from the diagram below in which we approximate the curve of probability into the shape of a triangle.

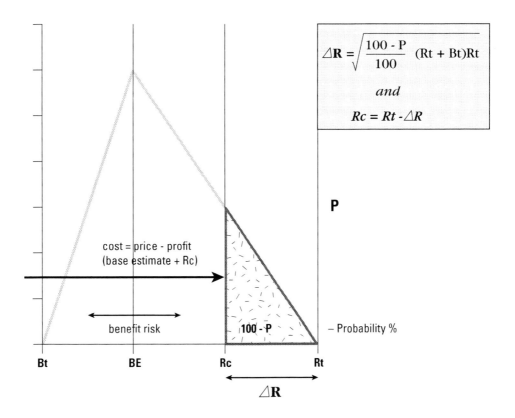

$$\triangle R = \sqrt{\frac{100 - P}{100}\ (Rt + Bt)Rt}$$

and

$$Rc = Rt - \triangle R$$

Figure 1: Corrected risk provision

The error introduced by this approximation has been demonstrated to be within the errors inherent in a subjective risk assessment and analysis procedure and the result is on the conservative side, i.e. a computerised smooth curve analysis would yield a lower Rc and therefore lower cost than the approximation, which is therefore 'safe'. The technique is so simple that any salesman operating thousands of miles from home can continually reassess the corrected risk provision Rc as the negotiation proceeds. As $Price = BE + Rc + Profit$, the salesperson can continually reassess the profit. Changes of scope will affect the value of BE and changes in the contract conditions will affect Rc but the probability of the break-even cost being $BE = Rc$ will remain at value P as set by the policy and used in the formula above. Alternatively you can look at the finally negotiated position in a different way. Concessions to the client will have reduced the profit due to reductions in the price and possibly increases in BE and Rc. Holding the profit at its original level and amending the BE, if the scope has changed, will leave a reduced value for the risk provision which we may call RD (adjusted risk provision). The adjusted probability Pa of breaking even on $BE + Ra$ is given in the formula at the bottom of the diagram. This probability will be lower than P and your management can make the decision as to whether it is acceptable before entering into a contract.

The consistency, competence and reliability of the technique has been demonstrated in practice and your organisation may find it can reduce the probability level which was set originally. Feedback from completed contracts and those under execution which have passed through the approval procedure, is vital and that is achieved through contract auditing.

Relationship of cost and price

It is a fact that the majority of businesses base their pricing on their costs. Of companies selling products to industry some 80% base their prices exclusively on a cost-based system. Whilst it is true that costs cannot be ignored, because overall prices must exceed costs in the long-term if an organisation is to stay in business, there is no reason why there should be a fixed link between costs and prices. After cost-based pricing systems the most common focus is on the pricing of competitors, of which competitive tendering is one example. The problem with this approach is that salesmen, who are the usual source of information about competitors' prices, will tend to drive prices down in order to increase their sales. Very few organisations conduct structured market studies to determine the best price to sell at.

Where prices are determined by non-cost factors some two out of three businesses never ask their customers what is acceptable in terms of price, but a little investigation work, especially before any tendering period starts, may reveal what the customer is expecting or prepared to pay. This in turn may indicate the level of profit that can be achieved, or may show up the need to reduce costs in order to be in with a chance.

When the purchaser thinks they can define their requirements fairly precisely and in such a way that several companies can provide what they require, they will call for competitive tenders. This makes the job of fixing the price very difficult and the single most important decision for the supplier – make no mistake, price is nearly always a critical factor in assessing tenders. This is not to say that the job will invariably go to the lowest bidder – purchasers will usually consider other factors. If you as the supplier believe that a number of prices will be similar it is important to think of other benefits of your chosen solution and to sell these to the purchaser. These may include more efficient operating costs, use of local labour, particular benefits for the environment, etc.

Profit

As mentioned earlier the level of profit to be built into the price is a commercial decision dependent on what the market will stand. In some markets it may be prudent to build in a negotiating margin which is there to be given away in negotiation. This is often needed in private sector projects overseas, particularly where successive rebids are anticipated. This allows the final negotiator on the client's side to demonstrate their competence by negotiating the price down whilst the contractor will preserve their authorised minimum profit level.

The authorised profit level may of course be negative where you must act aggressively to maintain your place in a traditional market or secure a place in a new market. It is easier for a sales executive to persuade the Board to subsidise the price when they have confidence that the level of risk provision gives a high probability of breaking even on the cost estimate and a good chance of turning risk provision into profit through competent risk management during contract execution. Where a contract is secured based on a negative profit particular attention must be paid to the competence of the project management through regular reviews and contract audits.

Some other aspects which must be considered before finalising the price are discussed below.

Inflation

Most proposals today require fixed prices unless the contract period is very extended. Therefore you must protect yourself against the effects of inflation, not only between the bid date and the date of contract effectiveness, but also through to the end of the secured contract. The limitation placed on the validity of the bid permits adjustment if there is undue delay on the client's part in placing the contract and bringing it into effect. For the execution period various elements of the estimate must be based on the contract programme. Man-hours may be expended over a period of several years and escalation must be applied to the man-hour cost estimate on a year by year basis on a best estimate of the inflation likely to occur.

The prices of vendors and subcontractors must have adequate validity to cover the time when the work is to be carried out. If this is not possible in-house estimates of the likely inflation must be added to the quoted prices. These estimates are of course examined in the risk analysis process.

In countries where inflation is high, such as Latin America, South Africa or Turkey, fixed prices for local works should not be bid. Firm prices should only be submitted as these are only fixed up to the bid submission date, after which they are escalated according to formulae which are accepted in the country of the project. These formulae are designed to take account of escalation in labour rates and material costs and they assume a portion of the contract cost is fixed (e.g. for profit margins, provisions and certain overheads). They are based on indices which are typically published monthly, although occasionally a quarterly index may be used.

A typical formula is shown in Figure 2 (page 53). The aim is to shift the bulk of the risk on inflation to the buyer. National indices are used – normally chosen to reflect the industry of the seller who is incurring the costs. If the seller's costs are contained within the national rate of inflation, a good clause will recoup the extra costs due to inflation for the seller.

The buyer normally assumes that over the period of the contract part of the price will remain fixed (e.g. profit). The formula shown in Figure 2 is based on 10% fixed – represented by 0.1 in the outer brackets. If a higher figure (e.g. 0.175 equivalent to a fixed portion of 17.5%) is negotiated, a lower increase from inflation will result.

The formula shown assumes that 60% of the seller's spend varies as the labour index and 40% as the materials index. The ratio of labour to material spend in the formula can be varied as required. In the example the seller's spend is made throughout the contract period. Hence the times T1 and T2 chosen for the indices are at midway points, chosen to give effectively average indices – e.g. after 18 months in a 24-month contract. T1 may be the same as T2.

A simple formula for inflation is:

$$P_D = P_0[0.1 + 0.9(0.6L_{T1}/L_0 + 0.4M_{T2}/M_0)]$$

where:

P_0 =   Price at time zero (i.e. base time such as contract date or tender date)

P_D =   Price at delivery

L_0 =   Chosen Labour index at time zero (i.e. base time)

L_{T1} =   Chosen Labour index at time T1 (to give effective average index)

M_0 =   Chosen Materials index at time zero

M_{T2} =   Chosen Materials index at time T2 (to give effective average index)

Figure 2: An inflation formula

If the contract is to be paid in instalments a similar formula can be used. In this case however each instalment (except the first if it is paid on order) will be calculated separately using the indices of the appropriate date – say three months before the instalment is due.

There is yet another problem for which we must cater. The publication of the indices is some time after the month to which they refer. It is quite probable that an instalment will fall due before the indices used in the formula for the appropriate date are known. It is common to arrange for the instalment to be paid in two parts, one when the instalment becomes due and the increment calculated from the formula payable (say) four months later, when the relevant indices have been published. You have to keep a careful check to ensure that such an incremental payment is not forgotten.

Other formulae are in use. BEAMA publish a series of formulae, which are commonly used for electrical and mechanical plant. One BEAMA formula increases the price by 0.475% per 1% difference between L0 (at tender or other agreed date) and the average of the labour indices over the last two-thirds of the contract period. The price also increases by 0.475% per 1% difference between M0 and the average of the material indices starting with that last published before the two-fifths point of the contract period and ending with that published immediately before the four-fifths point of the contract period. The labour index is defined as the BEAMA Labour Cost Index for Mechanical or Electrical Engineering as appropriate; the material index used is typically that for mechanical or electrical engineering materials published by the UK Government's National Statistical Office (NSO) in *'Monthly Digest of Statistics'*. Other indices should be substituted as appropriate and more specific price indices are found in the publication *'Producer Price Indices – MM22'*, again from the NSO.

Exchange risks

In recent years international contractors based in the UK have had to contend with considerable exchange rate risks. Overseas clients have required bids to be expressed in US dollars or Euros for the offshore content and frequently local currency for the onshore portion. Increasingly, organisations are facing demands to price in Euros, even for domestic customers.

Your expenditure is also likely to be in several currencies, as much of the equipment and even design services might have to be procured from such sources as Japan, Korea, China, Taiwan, Brazil and India in order to be competitive. Where such multi-sourcing is required the cost estimate must be broken down by currency and special steps taken to manage the risk. As the client is in control of the contract award date and the contract effectiveness date it is usually not possible to predict equipment delivery dates so as to apply forward exchange rates. Your greatest risk is between the bid submission date and the contract award date. At one time it was possible to take out 'Tender to Contract' cover at reasonable cost, but such cover is now expensive. It is therefore prudent to state in the proposal the amounts of the contract price which will be spent in various foreign currencies and the conversion rates used, then stipulate that, when the contract becomes effective, the price will be adjusted to take account of exchange rate movements. On contract award you can then enter into forward exchange contracts to provide for your future needs.

The general rule on currencies is to go for the hardest currency possible. Where a client insists on part of the bid being in a soft currency that component should be no greater than the estimated expenditure in that currency. If it is greater, then the excess must be built into the cost estimate as an extra hard currency cost

since the surplus in soft currency may not be convertible. The inclusion of a soft currency element may appear attractive to a client in a country with a soft currency, such as Morocco.

Credit insurance

Although it is a relatively rare occurrence it has been known for a client to default on a contract, by failing to pay in accordance with the terms of payment. This can have serious implications for you as the contractor particularly if the default persists. If there is any doubt about the client's ability to pay it is an essential part of the enquiry acceptance procedure and of the tender approval procedure to check their credit rating by reference to such agencies as Dun and Bradstreet. If this indicates a serious position the proposal should not proceed and no offer should be submitted. Even if you are satisfied at this stage it may be prudent to take protective measures. For UK contracts credit insurance is available but other methods can be adopted to secure payment. For export contracts the first step is to request 'Irrevocable Letters of Credit' and in some cases these should be confirmed through a first class bank. However, the most secure method is to take out credit insurance. The Dutch credit insurer NCM is the market leader for UK export contracts, having taken over the business from ECGD. The French insurer COFACE is also established in the UK and the Lloyds market can also provide credit insurance cover. Reduced premiums can be obtained if you are a regular exporter and undertake to insure all your export business with a given insurer.

Let us examine a typical NCM credit insurance. Risk is divided into pre-credit and credit risk. The former risk period is calculated from the date of contract up to the date of delivery. The premium is related to the length of this period, up to a maximum of 60 months. The latter risk period is from the date of delivery to the due date for payment and premium is related to this period, up to a maximum of 24 months. For each potential client you apply for a credit limit which becomes the insurer's maximum liability and if this is lower than the bid price you would be advised to reconsider whether to proceed with the proposal. The policy provides cover for 90% of the loss in respect of commercial risks related to the client and 95% of the loss in respect of political risks related to the client's country.

Customer-demanded financial constraints and information

Nominated vendors/subcontractors

These are nominated in the ITT by the client and this practice precludes the seeking of competitive tenders from vendors/subcontractors for the scope covered by the nomination. It can only be justified where the client has a long-term relationship with a vendor/subcontractor which guarantees value for money and/or standardisation of equipment leading to savings on spare parts/maintenance. It operates against the objective of securing the lowest price for the project. It can also lead to arguments on responsibility for failures to meet plant performance guarantees and failures during the defects liability period.

Sourcing preferences

These may be notified by a client whilst not going so far as to nominate vendors, and this can be a difficult issue. You will have to assume responsibility for any preferred suppliers or sub-contractors. However, you can secure an advantage during the adjudication procedure by responding to these preferences. A client may also make it clear that sourcing from certain companies or countries will not be accepted. This reduces your options but client wishes must be respected.

Bonds and guarantees

These are frequently requested by clients. The most serious effect is to limit a contractor's borrowing powers since they are treated as if they were an overdraft, as they can be called at any time, albeit unfairly. Bonds and guarantees also cost money to arrange and this cost must be included in the cost estimate. Bonds issued by local banks on export projects are much more expensive than those issued by UK banks. Typical bonds are as follows:

- **Bid bonds** – these have to be provided, if requested in the ITB, at the time of bid submission. They are usually for a small percentage of the bid price and are forfeited if you withdraw from the bidding procedure before a contract has been placed or the project is abandoned.

- **Downpayment bond** – this is for the value of the downpayment and reduces in value pro-rata to the value of the work done and goods delivered by you as the contractor.

- **Performance bond** – this relates to the obligations undertaken in the contract and usually remains valid until final acceptance of the plant.

- **Retention bond** – this is often required if the final retention payment is made by the client before your responsibilities have been completed. The cost of such a bond is usually much less than the interest which can be earned on retention monies released to you, yet the bond fully protects the client.

Project finance requirements

These are frequently required on major export contracts and can be up to 100% of the contract value. Where multi-currency procurement is involved this can cause you difficulty as it may limit your ability to procure from the cheapest source.

Terms of payment

These have a significant bearing on the bid price. If these are specified by the client in the ITT and are non-negotiable, careful assessment of the cash flow over the life of the contract must be made and if it is net negative then a financing cost must be built into the cost estimate thereby giving a higher price. Short-term troughs of cash flow penetration can be very large and cause you problems, particularly if several contracts have penetration at the same time. It is therefore essential to pass on the client's terms of payment to vendors/subcontractors and this may not always be possible. In any case it will increase the vendors' prices and therefore the cost estimate.

Pricing schedules

Client requirements in this area frequently do not match your work breakdown structure and therefore the cost estimate. Great care must be taken when rearranging the figures to meet the client's requirements. Once a contract is secured the conversion of the finally agreed prices into a cost control budget for the control of contract execution can also cause difficulty and delay. Careful control throughout the negotiation is therefore necessary if errors are to be avoided which could lead to losses.

Pricing conclusion

The following is a brief summary of the points to be considered when deciding on a price for the proposal. It is worth emphasising that:

- There is no substitute for a soundly based cost estimate and time spent in agonising over the profit level to be included, which probably constitutes only 1-5% of the price, is better spent examining the estimate and refining it. Any remaining areas of doubt should be assessed in the risk analysis.

- Risk provision is part of the cost estimate and must not be affected by the market situation.

- A reliable and well proven risk analysis technique will provide you with the confidence needed to permit an aggressive pricing policy with lower margins at the point of sale.

Writing your tender

chapter 7

Chapter 7:
Writing your tender

Writing at times can be a mundane business and when you sit with a blank piece of paper in front of you, with few thoughts in your head, then it is all pretty disheartening. Tenders have to be written and the words have to come from you. We have seen and realised in previous chapters that tenders are vital to business – good tenders mean good business. Tenders have to be written and they have to be good.

A good tender will lower the risk, your customer will understand immediately what you are trying to sell and therefore will not add in any contingency to your price to cover any unknowns or hidden risks to them. Good writing therefore has an enormous impact on the reception your tender gets with your customer, which in turn directly affects the future well being of your organisation.

A tender is a means of communication between you and your customer, transferring requirements from you to your customer. The primary way you do it is with words.

The words should describe that you understand your customer's needs and aims, that you are committed to their project and want to become part of their business growth. The words should also protect your company. The reader, your customer, wants to know what you intend to deliver, when you will deliver it, what quality and at what price. They want to feel confident that you'll perform and they also want to see that you are enthusiastic. Enthusiasm is contagious and it will help them sell you inside their company.

Making your customer's life easier

In your writing, the prime aim is to 'consider your reader'. They have to read the whole tender, and it may be a book a few inches thick! They will be a busy person, they cannot set aside the time to read it in one go. They will get interrupted, they will have to stop and concentrate on other matters from time to time. It is probable therefore that they will not read every word you write. They will sometimes scan the words, and it is up to you to help them not miss out the vital bits. If you consider them as you write, you will end up with a better and more readable tender.

Communications

The analysis and understanding of any form of communication can be related to the ideas put forward by Shannon in the late 40's, and writing certainly conforms. Shannon said that to communicate, you start with a sender. The information is then encoded, passes along a communications channel, is decoded and finally received. Noise always gets into the communications channel and too much noise corrupts the message.

In writing, the sender is the writer and their brain takes their concept, translates it into language and then they put it down in words. At the receiving end, the reader looks at this series of squiggles and tries to re-construct the original thoughts in their mind. How much easier it would be if we could use pictures, then these artificial carriers, i.e. the words, would be superfluous. However, we cannot do that all the time, we have to use words.

If you make a mistake in your encoding, or too much noise gets into the communication link, then the reader has no chance of deciphering the original thought. It is not surprising, therefore, that clarity and accuracy of thought are two of the main prerequisites of tender writing. Presenting a strong, clear and unambiguous tender helps prevent any noise affecting or modifying your messages.

You should spend lots of time and effort preparing your tender. Ideas, drafts, proof reading, correcting and all the other activities take up valuable resources. Your customer will take your tender, with the others from your competitors, and read them once. After this first read through, they may well produce a short list to study in greater detail.

You have to get on this short list and it has to be achieved after one read of the document. There's no appeal, you can't say that it is all made clear on page 74 – once it's been consigned to the bin, it stays there.

The words are therefore so important, poor ones will make your life difficult, while good ones will give you an inside edge.

For instance, if you are trying to explain something new or unfamiliar to the customer, start with something that is known and then introduce the unknown. You cannot communicate with anyone except in terms of their own experience.

The message from earlier is important, *consider your reader*. There is precious little reason for writing if it is not for the benefit of a reader, so put them first in your thoughts. Construct your document around what they want to know, the way they want to glean the information, and the best way for them to read it.

You also have to keep it simple and in so doing, keep the reader's interest. Give them time to assimilate what they have read. A couple of blank white lines tell your reader that they can pause before going on, that one particular message is finished and the next message is about to start.

You also need to keep it flowing, keep it logical. A jump jars the concentration – and then you've lost your reader.

Planning to write

The normal method of planning to write is applicable to writing specifications:

- Plan what you want to say

- Draft an outline

- Review the draft, with your boss, the specification manager, your colleagues, etc.

- Add any technical (or commercial) messages

- Write the first text

- Review this with others

- Then edit according to the comments.

Don't be proud, listen to other people's comments, just because they have different views doesn't mean that they are stupid. You may have gone off on a tangent and need pulling back. Make the revisions suggested.

Also arm yourself with good tools:

- A dictionary – we all make silly mistakes and spell checkers on computers often don't know about technical terms.

- A thesaurus – nowadays you can get them in A to Z format, rather than the traditional 'Roget' fashion; for engineers, this is far easier to use.

- Read other books about the use of English (*Fowler's Modern English Usage, Usage and Abusage* by Eric Partridge, *The Penguin Book of Troublesome Words*, are just a few).

The style for tenders

Directives for tender writing

An author needs directives to guide them in the way the company wants to go. The directives will come from a tender manager in the main and will address typically items such as:

- Key points and themes
- Storylines
- Performance, technology and personnel, as appropriate
- Commercial topics
- Presentation issues, charts and graphics
- Covering your own vulnerabilities and weaknesses
- Poisoning the competition.

The aim is to achieve a level of consistency throughout the document, especially if it is a very large one with many contributors. All writers should be using and incorporating the same messages.

Style

Style is influenced by a number of things – house style, corporate image, personality of the tender manager, whether the customer is new or an old friend etc. Generally however, the style to adopt in the absence of any of these influences should be:

- Factual and informative, clear and understandable
- Authoritative – you are not posing questions, you are giving a solution, and your solution will work first time
- Convincing and immediately believable; anticipate 'what if' questions from the customer, answer them in the tender
- Warm and possibly almost personal, not cloying but professional.

Navigating

Just as you would use the sequence of (i) a large-scale road map, (ii) looking at signposts and (iii) an A-Z of the town for finding your way in a new country, you need similar articles for navigating round documents.

The large scale road map, on one page for clarity and ease of use, is the list of contents; the signposts are the section titles and also the headers and footers at the top and bottom of the document; and an index equates to an A-Z. You may not want an index in a tender but the parallels for the other two are just as compelling. Remember, try to get your contents list on one page.

Plain simple words are the least misunderstood. Use them. With tenders, you should avoid trying to create a literary masterpiece – if you are not sure of the meaning of a word, then you will use it incorrectly. Avoid unfamiliar words.

Use short words and use short sentences. As a rule, short sentences work better.

Use the English of everyday conversation wherever possible. You can explain things better by using everyday speech because those are the words you are most familiar with. Clarity of thought precedes clarity of writing and if you are trying to use obscure words and phrases then these will only serve to obscure your thoughts.

Use words accurately; know the precise meaning of the words you are using. A tender will probably form part of a legal contract between you and your customer so it is as well, therefore, to try to avoid any form of conflict in the words. Accuracy avoids misunderstanding and misunderstanding will cost you money and time to put right later in the project. 'Say what you mean, and mean what you say' is quite a sensible slogan for tender writing.

What not to do

Irritations can upset your reader; but they may not alter the legal meaning of the tender. The true meaning of what you intend to deliver should be conveyed but the message should be conveyed in a way that doesn't rankle or offend the reader. However, it is as well to realise that simple errors can cause your reader to question the professionalism of you, the writer:

- Bad grammar, poor spelling, silly punctuation
- Meaningless phrases, awkward construction of sentences
- Stilted prose, Latin and Greek words/phrases
- American spelling and phrases (unless you are going for a very American contract!)
- Convoluted sentences with ambiguous meanings
- Pomposity, arrogance, sloppiness.

Using plain English

Spelling

Spelling has been described as 'one of the decencies of life' and certainly a misspelt document is a sure way of raising the eyebrows of the reader. If there are too many, they may very well give up reading and throw it away.

Even with increasing reliance being placed on spell checkers in word processors, errors can become embedded in a document. It is important though to realise that there are some words that have to be spelt correctly. There are pairs of words similarly spelt but with different meanings, you have to get them right, for example:

- Discreet and discrete

- Hangar and hanger

- Lightning and lightening.

This is another reason for having a dictionary on your desk.

Punctuation

The function of punctuation is to make crystal clear the meaning of your writing. If you mix up full stops, commas and semicolons, then you are not getting your thoughts clear, your mind is muddled. Pay particular attention to punctuation.

Apostrophes are probably the most misunderstood punctuation today. They have very specific uses and if you don't know what they are for, then never use them. It is far less of a crime to miss them out than to put them in the wrong places. Misplaced apostrophes always get a laugh when they are spotted.

Commas can lead to misunderstandings, especially if they are put in the wrong places in sequences of adjectives and related nouns. Just watch out for them. If it is not clear, break it down into a number of short sentences.

Paragraphs

A paragraph is for one topic. It therefore can be one line long or twenty lines long. In a tender, if you put two topics in one paragraph, you run the risk of the customer accepting one half but not the other, with the subsequent difficult task of deciding exactly what you think you are supplying. One half of such a paragraph may be compliant with the customer's specification and the other half not. The customer then has to sort out whether you are, or are not, acceptable on the issue.

The key statement of a paragraph should be its first sentence. The reader can then read it and either like what they have seen and read the whole paragraph or have no interest in the topic and skip the rest. It also helps them to jump back into a paragraph if the first glance tells them where they are.

For tenders, the first sentence of a paragraph should make a claim and the remainder of the paragraph should substantiate the claim. A claim is a benefit for the customer, the substantiation is a feature of your product. Every claim must be substantiated; features without benefits are worthless.

Lists of items are a sensible way of organising information in tenders. They help you when you try to check that nothing has been left out and they help the reader, your customer, to make sure all is clear and according to the specification. There are many lists in this text and you can see for yourself if you understand the message.

Verbs

A customer in his specification will use the verb 'shall' to denote mandatory requirements which have to be strictly followed in order to conform to the customer's requirements and no deviations are allowed. 'Should' indicates a recommendation and 'may' shows permission, both have places in specifications.

Tenders are promises and the verb to convey this idea is 'will'. If in part of the tender you require the customer to do something, like deliver drawings, then use 'shall' to convey that this is a mandatory requirement to achieve timely completion of the task.

Abbreviations

Define these fully the first time you use them and make a glossary of all abbreviations used. Correlation of the indices from various writers and contributors, especially in other departments, helps prevent the same abbreviation being used for two or more different phrases. Place the Glossary in your tender.

The perils of word processors

Modern technology in the office is so clever that you can easily be dazzled by it. There are problems in using it and you should be aware of them:

- Not checking other people's text when you download it onto your document

- Cross referencing to paragraphs that no longer exist

- Leaving sensitive data on commonly accessible hard disks

- Because it is easy, calling for draft after draft; you need to be strict with yourself and limit the drafts you run off

- Watch out for automatic hyphenation changing the meanings of words. A 'keyboard decision' asks what key do I press? A 'key-board decision' could be a new company policy!

Writing

In essence, therefore, writing tenders is an exercise in using plain, simple, unambiguous English. Clarity of writing a tender follows clarity of your thoughts. Use familiar words. Avoid abstract nouns wherever possible. Use Anglo-Saxon words rather than flamboyant Latin and Greek expressions. Don't use extravagant adjectives, pretentious phrases or hackneyed expressions. Keep away from jargon and clichés. Don't get confused by similar types of word. Use dictionaries and books on English to help you.

Good ideas deserve good tenders. Don't let a poor description devalue or deface your innovations.

Clarity, completeness and consistency

What, therefore, does the reader want from you? Primarily they want help of one sort or another.

- They want to be reminded where they are in the document – good, meaningful titles are useful here

- They want summaries

- They want the information in digestible portions

- They want paragraphs headed by topic sentences so they can decide whether they need to read on or skip something

- They need to have very important bits standing out so they are recognisable

- They want to get overviews of what the whole document is and what it contains

- They need to be able to find where bits of information are.

Essentially readers want help from you, the writer. You can generally give it without any extra effort. Consider what your reader wants, let that be a driving force when you write.

Trade names and proprietary items

Be very wary of trade names that are used in enquiry documents. For much of the time this is when purchasers are lazy and use a trade name when they are prepared to accept any equivalent alternative. For example, if you are bidding for a cleaning contract, requirements to use a 'Hoover' almost certainly mean any vacuum cleaner. However, there will be times when the purchaser means what they say and if you offer something else in your tender you may become non-compliant. If in doubt which applies, ask! Most purchasers will be only too happy to clarify their enquiries, because this means they will receive better tenders.

You must also think before you offer specific trade names in your tender. Do so only when you genuinely intend to supply that make of item. Remember, the tender becomes a contract and the purchaser will expect you to deliver exactly what is specified. Sometimes a trade name is the normal way of describing a generic product in a particular industry. If this is the best way of saying what is included in your offer, remember to add the words 'or equivalent' if that is what you really mean. Restricting yourself to a specific make of equipment reduces your options if the model is withdrawn or the manufacturer goes out of business or merges with another. Obviously, if your offer depends on a proprietary item or process then say so, especially if that adds credibility to your offer.

Putting your tender together

chapter 8

Chapter 8:
Putting your tender together

The contents of a proposal document

This chapter of the Report deals with how to organise your proposals and what types of information you should include. The actual writing of the text is covered in the previous chapter. It tells you how to arrange what you have to say in a logical fashion that will help your client understand what you have to offer, with the minimum effort on his/her part.

Don't produce a proposal in isolation. Find out what your client wants in terms of the amount of detail. If you don't know, ask them. You want to give them what they expect. Sometimes, your client will tell you how to lay out your proposal, or even give you schedules to complete. Don't try to improve on their layout – just follow the instructions given. Failure to comply will result in your bid being marked down, even if only sub-consciously.

However, if your client leaves it open as to how the tender is to be presented, or has asked you to make a proposal, you have much more freedom over how you lay your documentation out. Develop a house style that suits your products or services, the type of organisation you are, the image you are trying to project and follow that. It is not a bad idea to produce a master proposal document which covers all the points you want to get across and, of course, the advantages to your customers in using you rather than the competition.

Sections

Your client wants to know when he reads your proposal:

- What are they going to get?
- When are they going to get it?
- How much are they going to have to pay?

These questions are answered in the sections dealing with technical, management and commercial matters respectively.

There should also be a summary to give an overall view of what the customer is being offered and this is often called the executive summary. In smaller proposals it might simply be called the introduction.

Larger proposals may well have each section bound separately. Even in smaller projects it is often a good idea to make each section clearly separable, because the customer may well split their assessment of your bid between a number of different individuals or departments. Again, make sure you follow any explicit instructions concerning how the document is put together, since the customer may well wish to copy particular sections, which becomes difficult if you have used some patented glue binding!

Executive summary

For anything but the smallest proposals a summary overview should be included at the beginning of the proposal. This is particularly important if the proposal is being presented to a new client. This overview is often given the name 'executive summary'. It should cover all the key points in the proposal and should be aimed at senior executives. Those people are too busy to read all the details, but they need to receive the impression that you have the necessary expertise, financial backing, management capabilities and resources to handle the job. They should not come away with any doubts in their minds on these issues.

You therefore have to demonstrate that you understand the client's needs and that you have an achievable, value for money, low risk solution to the customer's requirements.

The overview should be written by a senior person, and should not be delegated to a junior manager. It must be brief and to the point and each paragraph should cover a different key issue.

Remember that it may be copied on its own, without the rest of the bid, to other decision makers within the client's organisation, so make sure your own organisation is clearly identified within it.

Technical section

The ideal technical section demonstrates total understanding of the customer's needs. It has to convince the customer that it will deliver the results promised. It should be completely compliant with what the customer wants. Ideally, it should play back the customer's preferred solution. This is not the time or place to be innovative – if you know that your customer wants a particular piece of kit or way of doing things then offer that, not something else.

71

Showing that you understand what the customer requires depends on what they have given you – a full formal specification or merely a telephone request. If you have a full specification document, you need to explain how you have interpreted it, confirm that you have included any clarification received subsequently and then describe the technical basis for your bid. If, on the other hand, you have only received a brief verbal request, you should list the customer's requirements and objectives as you see them. Include what they are likely to achieve from what you are offering them. If you don't know, ask them. If you still don't know you are probably wasting your time.

You then need to describe what you are offering the customer, whether this is plant, services, works, software or facilities. Your main solution must be compliant with their requirements. If you feel you have a better solution which is non-compliant this should be included as an alternative offer, not a replacement for what the customer thinks they need.

You may need to explain how you arrived at your main solution. If necessary, explain your method of working, the main sub-contractors you will use, and any innovations that you believe confirm your ability to achieve the desired results, but do be careful not to raise questions in the customer's mind.

Your prime offer should be just adequate for the job. This encourages the customer to believe they will be getting value for money. When you review your proposal before finally issuing it you must remove any frills or gold knobs that have been designed in.

Your offer may well require input from the customer – perhaps special tooling or strategic spare parts. You may require facilities that the customer owns. You will almost certainly require information and possibly approval from the customer to what you are doing. You must spell out in your proposal what you require and when. It may be useful to keep a checklist of what you normally require or the timescales you normally work to, and to include this, or extracts from it, but do remember to keep this under review to allow for changed circumstances.

When you are tendering to new clients or for new types of work, it may be useful to have another type of checklist. In order for you to be compliant your offer must be complete and the list will help ensure that you do not omit anything. You could include items under the following headings for example:

- Spares, maintenance, guarantees, warranty

- Quality requirements (BS EN ISO 9000)

- Safety

- Training

- Operational factors

- Environmental impact

- Security

- Disposal of equipment

- Public liability.

If you want to know what to include in the list, ask your customers what was omitted from previous proposals. This not only validates the checklist, but also demonstrates to your customers that you are trying to improve your performance.

You also need to include the technical messages you wish to put across. They should reflect what is best for the project and may include:

- The best technical solution, the best plant, the most skilled workforce

- The low risk of the proposed solution

- The soundness of the design

- The thoroughness of the analysis done

- The logic of your approach.

Management section

This is the section of a proposal that most often gets omitted, which loses business, because it is this section which convinces your client that you are able to manage the project successfully. You need to cover quality, programme and control. You want the client to feel confident that you can be relied on to get on with the job without giving them problems.

Quality can be demonstrated by referring to the relevant standards, most notably the ISO 9000 series, but you may need to say more in the light of what you know about the customer. Explain the ways in which you are spreading the quality message throughout the whole of your organisation. If you have a total quality management policy spell out what it contains. If you run quality circles explain this. But do make sure that you have dealt with all previous concerns if you are tendering to an existing customer. If necessary, get feedback from them on how they viewed previous projects. Also make sure that, if you are promoting a quality image, this includes the presentation of your tender documentation, the way in which telephone calls are handled, the reliability of message taking, etc.

Project programmes are best covered in charts. Bar charts can be very effective, but ensure that the information on them corresponds with the technical

description. More complex programmes may require the submission of other charts, such as PERT diagrams, although these more detailed documents will often follow the award of contract. If you are concerned to cover response times for a continuous service, then you may simply need to state the service levels offered.

Don't be afraid to state the obvious. If you can meet required delivery dates, say so. Silence may be assumed to mean non-compliance. If you can better the required delivery, make sure this is of benefit to your customer before offering it – it may just present them with an additional problem. If you can't meet the delivery, again say so – customers always prefer to know the worst as early as possible, and it may well be that they have requested the impossible. Remember you are looking to gain a successful contract, and promising an impossible response will only lead to problems during the contract.

If you are being asked to accept liquidated damages, be very careful about what you are offering and the rate and extent of the damages you are prepared to accept.

The third topic for the management section is the question of control. Personnel, skills, equipment and management all should be mentioned to convince your client that you can do the job. Identify the main sub-contractors you will be using and consider getting them to contribute to the proposal.

It may be appropriate to describe your organisation in so far as it is relevant to the project. You may include CVs of key personnel, but remember they are selling CVs, not job-seeking CVs. Only include the details that are relevant.

After reading the management section you client should be convinced that you are a well-organised management team, where each component knows its place and is under the necessary control.

Commercial section

This part of the proposal needs to show your customer that you are offering the best commercial deal. Make sure here, as in other sections of the proposal, that you are describing something special to your organisation. If the competition offers a better deal than you in some respects don't dwell too long on those items! So in order to avoid highlighting an aspect in which you are not strongest you have to be aware of the competition's strengths as well as their weaknesses.

The commercial section needs to cover:

- pricing

- payment

- terms and conditions

- other relevant factors.

You should address only matters of interest to the customer. For example, the financing of a £50,000 job is unlikely to be an issue, whereas it probably does need to be mentioned for a £25,000,000 project.

Of course the most important part of a proposal is generally the price and you need to think about how to present this. If you have a definite specification then you must quote the full price for meeting that specification. If you wish to offer alternatives (probably reductions) then do this in conjunction with options put forward in the technical section. On the other hand, if you have a functional or target specification to meet, then put your lowest price first and justify that. If this offer complies strictly with the stated requirements then say so. Desirable features can then be offered at an additional price.

Throughout the pricing section keep referring to the technical section and make it as easy as possible for your customer to correlate the two. As this is likely to be the most read part of the proposal, don't lose the opportunity to sell your offer here.

After the price you must spell out when you expect your client to pay you. Failure to do this leads to inevitable conflict later in the job. You may well have been told when you can expect to be paid and you need to think twice before requesting any amendment to this – the customer may load your offer disproportionately if they think that you are going to cause them administrative difficulties. You must also be realistic – clients will have payment systems, look at industry norms and their own cash flow position in determining when you actually get paid. Your pricing must reflect what you know about the likelihood of being paid in line with the stated terms.

Other factors to consider about payment are:

- how (electronically, cheque, bankers' draft, goods in kind, etc.)

- in what currency

- where

- documentation required (e.g. Engineer's certificates)

- the retentions to be held

- risk of non-payment.

These become particularly important in dealing with overseas customers.

Next you should mention terms and conditions – anathema to most salesmen! Typical of the topics to be covered here are:

- delivery of parts from your customer and the impact of delays

- approval of drawings/programmes/specifications by the customer or their Engineer and the timescales required

- delivery arrangements to your customer

- who owns any resulting intellectual property

- confidentiality of information and publicity

- where and when ownership changes hands

- when and where risk passes from one party to the other

- force majeure

- how, when and where acceptance of the work or plant or services is to be signified

- whether the contract can be varied, how, and to what extent

- dispute resolution/arbitration arrangements

- which country's law applies

- how long your offer remains open for acceptance

- special provisions for overseas contracts, especially who is arranging import/export documentation, permits, letters of credit, transport, shipping, etc.

In all sections of your proposal it is most important to be very clear about what you are offering and what you expect from your client. You must be consistent between sections, concise and unambiguous. The proposal must be as easy to read as possible so use plain English. Legalese or jargon may not be understood and if the client does not understand your offer that leaves them with a question mark.

Covering letters and other materials

Your proposal should be complete in itself and therefore any covering letter should be kept very brief and to the point. It should refer to the relevant correspondence from the customer and should also list any other materials enclosed, such as general sales brochures, reference portfolios, photographs, and videos. These documents need to be marked individually as being part of the package and all should bear your organisation's name.

Do find out again what your customer expects from you. If they have issued formal tender documentation, that may be all that they want returned. The normal place for general sales literature is before you get onto the tender list. Try to fit the material enclosed with what is expected.

Presentation and appearance

The physical size of the document to be presented does not necessarily relate to the value of the contract – this will largely be determined by the customer's instructions and expectations. However, your proposals should always be presented professionally in order to gain respect.

Your proposal is going to be read, so you must help the reader as much as possible. The reader needs an indication of where they are and how far they have to go. You should therefore give them:

- titles that have meaning

- headers and footers that give positive guidance of where you are in the document

- key sentences, stating your claims, heading each paragraph.

Being consistent helps the reader considerably. Try to keep to one style of headings, diagrams and text throughout the whole document. A common format should be used for most, if not all, of the text. If you are preparing a series of proposals, then the same guidelines should be followed.

Consider an appropriate binding for the document. Pages must lie flat and will often need to be photocopied, so any fancy glue binding is probably not appropriate. Simple staples may suffice for a small tender. For larger proposals a ring binder is often a good choice.

Consider what you should include on the front cover. Remember this is the first thing your customer will see. This may be dictated by your organisation's policy or by the customer's instructions. Otherwise consider:

- the project name
- a project photograph, sketch or drawing
- your organisation's name
- a statement of what the document is, i.e. 'A bid for ....'
- a reference number of the document.

After the cover comes the first page with real information. Again this may be fixed by the customer or by your own house style, but consider including the following:

- references: organisation's name, what the document is, what project it refers to, any cross references to other proposals, the enquiry reference and the document's own reference number
- quality assurance: issue number and date of issue, whether it is a controlled copy, if so, whose copy it is, name and signature of the author or proposal manager, name and signature of the person who authorised it
- name and address of the technical person for questions, the same for commercial questions
- confidentiality: statement of the level of security and who can copy it
- copyright: what restrictions are placed on the information as it is presented.

Remember that your proposal is copyright material. You do not need to put anything on the document but if you wish to retain copyright, a statement claiming ownership is worth making.

Often the information in a proposal is proprietary. If you want to protect your information, a suitable sentence should be included such as the following:

> 'The information contained in this tender is to be considered proprietary information. It shall not be reproduced, disclosed or used without prior written permission of (your organisation).'

You may then want to include a contents page listing what is included in the proposal and the order in which it is laid out. This is obviously more important for larger proposals.

Then you may want to consider an introduction. This is a statement of the objectives and is useful to give the reader guidance as to why the document has been produced. The Scope defines the extent and limitations of the proposal and lists any restrictions, exclusions or limits to its use. Both of these have their uses and can be properly employed on large proposals. In smaller tenders, having both can be an overkill.

A very effective feature is the 'message' from the Managing Director or Chief Executive. This is most important for large jobs or for significant new customers. It is there to stress enthusiasm, willingness and commitment from the top. Generally it need only be three or four paragraphs long but it should be signed, and by the person in whose name it is written.

For some jobs consider including a glossary of terms, abbreviations, etc. This may be especially useful if you are sending a proposal overseas, where the first language is not English. Alternatively, this can be included as an appendix at the end of the proposal.

Then you should include the three main sections discussed above: technical, management and commercial.

Adding spice

You can always improve on your presentation. You are looking for ways to make your presentation more appealing to your customer, but you must be careful not to go too far and put them off. A number of companies submit such expensive documentation that many clients immediately think they will be too costly and rule them out.

You must make sure that you fit the project concerned and fulfil the needs of your customer. You have to use a bit of show to distinguish yourself from the competition, but this must be done in a controlled manner. What you need to do is largely dictated by the type of organisation you are and the type of project you are tendering for. The suggestions that follow will in the main apply to proposals where you have the say in the presentation.

Look at the front cover of your proposal and consider whether you can use a bit of colour. Colour ink jet printers are very reasonable these days. You may be able to put some sort of photograph or drawing on the front cover. The cost is minimal but the effect is dramatic. Consider incorporating your customer's logo or their project logo, but make sure that they do not object first. Perhaps use a stylistic sketch of the ultimate application. Remember, your proposal will need to be sold inside your customer's organisation right up to the Board and first impressions count.

Consider putting some form of identification down the spine of the binder if space allows. This will help it stand out in a bookcase and keeps your name continually in the customer's mind.

Consider the appropriate paper size. Europeans expect A4 – it's what their photocopiers handle, but Americans may expect their standard sizes.

As for the text, this covers the typeface and the layout. Choose both with care. A two or three page bid can be successfully presented using a common typewriter font and layout. On the other hand a 100-page proposal will need to take account of the potential reading fatigue.

A multiplicity of fonts, in a multiplicity of sizes, multiple columns, graphic inserts and the advent of cheap desktop publishing have opened up many possibilities for layout. However with them come potential new problems.

Become familiar with what you have available in-house, and become familiar with how to use the facilities. There is a tendency to use all these new facilities at the same time, but this is a mistake. It is better to stay with one type style with a limited number of sizes in one document and restrict the number of different typefaces used in a document.

Proportional spacing allows more characters on a line, but beware that too many characters to a line can cause the reader to misread. 60-65 characters per line of text should be a maximum. Using multiple columns can overcome this. Two columns is the best choice as three columns can often produce awkward hyphenations and may constrain the length of your titles. Titles should not be allowed to flow over two lines.

Derive a set style for the layout of the document such that all sections appear consistent. Typically you could specify:

Section titles:	18 point and centred
Headings:	14 point, bold and left justified
Text:	12 point and justified

Consider incorporating graphics into the text. This has the added advantage of breaking up the text, making it easier to take in, and allowing the text to reinforce the graphics. If you are producing CVs in the management section, you might use photographs inserted into the text. If you have a tame graphic artist, consider using him to draw thumbnail sketches of the people involved in the project.

Your major selling points should be highlighted and one of the best ways of doing this is by using boxes inserted into the text. Inserts are the parts of the text which are initially read and will be read by those who are just skimming the document.

Look at various magazines to see how they do it. The PC magazines use this technique frequently to good effect. Other magazines which reflect the latest fashions in layout and text design are the magazines of the Sunday papers and the weekend editions of the dailies. Study these and extract ideas which catch your eye. Also look at company reports for various large public companies. These are generally expensively produced (with a few notable exceptions) using the latest designs, graphics, etc. They are examples of what is in fashion at the moment in business and can be an excellent source of ideas. Your customer's annual report can also indicate the style that will appeal in your proposal to them.

Pictures convey far more information than words and should be actively encouraged. A graphic artist is a very useful addition to a proposal writing team. Imagination and innovation should be allowed but you must keep the correct tone throughout the document. A proposal is a serious document and control must be retained.

The use of cartoons can be effective, but this is a more tricky area. This very much depends on the customer and on how well you know them. If there is any doubt then best leave cartoons alone.

Colour in graphics and photographs can be a positive addition. Make sure though that you supply enough copies to your customer. If they have to make copies themselves, the colour originals you supply will stay in a drawer while muddy black and white photocopies will be the ones circulated to the Board.

The executive summary is the one part of your proposal which will be read in full by your client's decision-makers. Treat it therefore as something special. Consider making it a separate document. A more glossy presentation with many graphics in it could be the best way for some customers. For substantial jobs, a short video could be made. Alternatively, consider a multimedia presentation on computer, but make sure the customer can use it – standards are still not uniform in this area!

Video is often seen as having an enormous price tag, but it need not be so. A short video can have great impact; it is a superb communications medium. The video can have certain stock sections about your company with suitable inserts relating to the proposal. It can tell your story and can be tailored to highlight your strengths. It can show your facilities in the most favourable light. It can illustrate the major points of your proposal and it will show your customer that you are one jump, at least, ahead of the competition.

More pizzazz can be added to your proposal in a variety of ways and it is up to you to work out the best for your client. Keep up-to-date with the latest graphic trends, see what others are doing and adapt it to your particular needs. Your document is a reflection of your organisation's image and you can use some of the techniques above to promote what you are and what you are selling.

Presentations and review

chapter **9**

Chapter 9:
Presentations and review

These days it is highly likely that you will be asked to make a presentation about your tender following submission of the formal documents. As purchasers' requirements become more complex some post-tender discussion is necessary to clarify exactly what your bid covers. Purchasers are under increasing financial pressure and are always seeking to find that bit extra. It is therefore essential to understand how to get the best from a presentation.

Preparing for a formal presentation

When you are asked to make a formal presentation find out as much as possible about the arrangements as early as possible:

- the time and place

- what facilities are available

- whether you can get into the room in advance to rehearse

- how many presentations will be made that day

- who will be in the audience, and what their particular interests are

- what your customer is seeking to gain from the presentation.

You then need to prepare your presentation. Aim to speak for a maximum of half the time available, allowing the rest for questions. Do not simply repeat your tender, but highlight the unique benefits of your solution.

See if you can determine when you make your presentation. All things being equal it is generally reckoned that it is best to go first (to set the standard) or last (to be in the most recent memory of the audience). However, you may not be given any choice. If you have the opportunity to rehearse your presentation in the actual room, take it. If necessary, ask if you can use the room the day before for rehearsal. If you cannot rehearse in the room itself, rehearse in as similar a location as you can find, and make sure you draft people in to act as the audience.

Decide who will be in your team and make sure they each have a role. This can be difficult if you have included experts in the team in case particular technical questions are asked, but who are not good at making presentations. If the presentation team cannot learn enough about the subject to answer immediate

questions, ensure that your technical experts receive presentation training. Remember, you can always give yourself the option to come back to your customer with technical information, provided you promise to do this promptly (and keep to your promise). Don't forget that it is as important to listen as to speak, so ensure that a team member is briefed to watch for responses in your audience. These will not just be verbal responses, but also body language and other visual clues.

Successful presentation techniques

When it comes to the presentation itself, remember that making presentations comes close to death, divorce and moving house in raising stress levels. Therefore reduce the stress on the team and build-up their confidence by ensuring that the presentation is well rehearsed. Be sure that everyone knows why your tender will succeed. When you enter the room or greet your audience (if you are there first), act confidently by keeping your back straight. Greet your audience with an outstretched hand. Maintain a lingering eye contact with them as you greet. Try to convey a quiet confidence with the first words you use.

Think about your body language, especially with the use of your hands. Outstretched arms pose a problem, an upward pointing finger conveys that you are telling your audience the solution to the problem (but make sure that you do not convey aggression by overuse of this gesture). Hands clasped together indicate that you are thinking about the problem posed while putting your hand on your chin indicates that you are listening actively to what the customer is saying to you. Don't confuse this with a hand in front of your month which indicates that you are lying or at least very uncertain about what you are saying.

Don't be afraid to use the power of your voice. Don't speak too fast, give the audience time to take in what you are saying. Pauses can be used to good effect, particularly to let an important message sink in. Use light and shade to vary the tone of your voice, learn to stretch and emphasise words.

Ensure that you have someone who can maintain control of the presentation itself. Your customer may decide at the last minute that you have less time than originally allocated, so someone must decide which parts of your prepared material to skip. Your customer may inform you of particular points they want to be covered. The person in charge of your team must then decide who will answer those points, but he or she should be skilled enough to buy some time for the designated individual to collect their thoughts.

The presentation should be very clear. Try to concentrate on no more than two-four key points or message nuggets. The presenters must also be consistent in the messages they give. These messages must be woven into the overall presentation and should concentrate on the unique benefits of your offer to the customer.

If you have time, support your messages with facts and figures to back them up. These can include statistics, especially if they come from independent sources, other opinions of relevant experts or authorities, analogies with similar circumstances, and personal experience, especially common experiences which the audience are likely to have had.

Try to keep your audience awake. If they are asleep mentally, you are wasting your time. Use memorable sound bites where appropriate – follow the example of politicians, however corny this may seem. Change audio/visual techniques (if appropriate) or change speakers. If you are confident, use drama or humour, but be especially careful with audiences from other countries and cultures. Use the language of everyday conversation to engage your audience's active participation. Make sure you keep using that positive body language and smile regularly at your audience.

Consider using visual aids but bear in mind the circumstances of the presentation. The higher the technology, the greater the potential impact, but also the greater the risk of something going wrong. Remember that if your presentation time is limited, setting up the technology can waste valuable minutes. Even if you are relying on simple overhead slides ensure that a good projector is available. If the model you are presented with is dim and dusty, cut your losses and make the presentation without slides. However, slides do act as a useful prompt to speakers and can help present statistical messages very effectively. If you use slides you should leave copies behind with the audience to remind them of what you have said. Sometimes a simple flipchart may be most effective and it is important not to forget how powerful physical props can be. Remember that any visual aids should support your message not get in the way. A common mistake with PowerPoint slides is to use a multitude of fancy effects and colour schemes so that the audience becomes mesmerised by the effect rather than the message.

In structuring your presentation it is no bad idea to follow the preacher's formula: tell them what you are going to say, say it, then tell them what you have said. If you are a team, introduce the team and explain the role of each person. If one person is there only to answer particular technical questions make sure this is clear. Otherwise they may appear as a wallflower and you will give the impression of having far too many staff.

In order to overcome nervousness, make sure that you know your subject matter and that you rehearse your presentation as many times as possible. Make sure that you arrive early at the presentation venue and check the facilities. There is nothing worse than arriving at the last minute and finding you have no time to collect your thoughts. If you are still nervous practice a few relaxing exercises before the presentation. Take a deep breath, hold it for a few seconds and then slowly exhale. Before you start speaking establish firm eye contact with the audience and don't think of them as hostile or challenging, but as eager to hear what you have to say. Remember they have arranged the presentation to learn more about your tender, so they want you to be as calm and organised as possible. They are waiting for you to interest them. If there is someone in the audience who is smiling at you or nodding at what you are saying then focus on them for the first minute of your presentation. This will give you confidence. But do remember to focus on everyone present during your presentation.

Often when we are speaking we make silly mistakes. We may get someone's name or job title wrong, or we may even refer to our audience by the name of some other organisation we were addressing the day before! If you make a mistake, then correct it immediately. This has the effect of changing potential embarrassment into sympathetic admiration for you. After all, many, if not all, in your audience will have been in the same situation, and they are just glad it is not them having to make the presentation. Make your audience smile at your mistake. Dealing with the blunder rather than ignoring it removes any impression that you are a fool.

Make sure that you demonstrate a clear understanding of the problem facing your customer and focus on your experience in the client's industry or for your client itself. Mention any significant accomplishments your organisation or team has achieved, and, in any case, give the background of the team, especially where it is relevant to the tender in hand.

It often helps to pause and look at your audience before you start speaking, but only if you are not too nervous. Do look round at your audience and never ignore anyone in the room. Try to address your remarks to everyone. Never ignore any opposition to what you are saying – at the least, refer to the fact that there seems to be some disagreement to what you are saying and make a point of dealing with it as soon as your prepared talk has finished. If you can, it is better to deal with it instantly. Watch for body language which may indicate support for what you're saying as well as opposition.

If you are in a team support each other, not least by paying attention to what your colleagues are saying. If you are bored because you have heard them dozens of time before, make sure you do not show it. If the audience detects you are bored they will be encouraged to switch off too. If you have a large audience, use bigger and slower gestures than if you are speaking to a small group.

Once you have made your main points always end on a positive note, with a key statement about why you are the best team or organisation to solve your customer's problem, and remember, it does no harm by positively asking for the business.

As I mentioned before, the most important part of any presentation for a tender is usually the question and answer session. It is as important to prepare for this as for your formal presentation. You must think of all the difficult questions that might be thrown at you and rehearse the answers. Even if they are never asked, knowing you have some answers ready will boost your confidence immeasurably. When you are being asked a question listen carefully to what is being said. There may be clues to what your audience's real concerns are or there may be a hidden question. Try to answer both if you can.

It is a good idea to acknowledge the question being asked, if you can by rephrasing it. This gives you more time to think of the answer and checks that you have understood the question properly. If you are being asked a question which you will cover a bit later, say that you will be covering that topic and that you will deal with the question at the time. Invite the questioner to remind you in case you forget. If the question is best answered by a colleague invite them to speak, but give them some time to think by rephrasing the question to check that you understand what is being asked.

If it is a difficult question, pause to demonstrate that it needs some thought, even if you have a rehearsed answer on the tip of your tongue. Some questions are simple and just need a quick answer. Some are complicated and require more thought. Some are loaded questions and you need to deal with the underlying issue. You will not know the answer to every question that may be asked. If this is the case, don't make up an answer, but promise to get back to the questioner as soon as you get back to the office. Make sure that you do get back to the questioner.

Once you have given your answer confirm with the questioner that you have answered their question fully (or as best you can). It may be that they really meant to ask a different question and this gives them the opportunity to get rid of the doubts in their mind.

Follow-up and debriefing

After any presentation it is worth doing an internal de-brief to hear from your colleagues what they think went well and what went badly. If there are areas which need strengthening before the next presentation make sure that you plan to undertake the necessary training or practice.

More importantly, you need to find out what the client thought about the presentation and whether there are still any unanswered questions or missing information. In general, your customer is likely to be in touch with you fairly quickly if yours is the bid most likely to win, but not invariably. A couple of days after the presentation (you do not want to approach your customer too quickly) it would be quite reasonable for you to contact your customer to ask if there are any further questions to be answered or information which would be helpful. The response will give you an idea of your chances. If you know that the customer is receiving other presentations you should wait until these are all over before making contact. If you have someone on your team who has a good relationship with someone on your customer's team try to arrange a meeting for a more thorough debriefing. Accept that this may have to wait until the customer has set up their contract.

You want as much information as possible about your bid – what were the strengths and weaknesses and how did these compare with the competition. It is worth working through a checklist, covering the technical aspects, the commercial aspects, the culture of your two organisations, personalities and so on. Even if you win the contract, it is worth asking for such a de-briefing, so that you can confirm what your strengths are.

If you have not been successful don't close the door on your customer. Make a note to make contact a few months into the new contract. Say you hope the contract is proving successful, but remind them that you are still around, still keen to seek their business and ask if there is anything else you can do to help them. This way you are preparing the ground for the next tender, or you may be in a good position to gain some additional work which, for whatever reason, is not going to your competitor.

Successful negotiations

When it comes to negotiating a tender it is important to keep in mind the different techniques of persuasion. They include:

- Using logical argument

- Using power and coercion

- Compromise

- Mutually advantageous concessions

- Emotion

- Understanding genuine business objectives

- Bluff or lies.

These techniques can be used by either or both parties, so be on the lookout for the other party to use them against you. Some of them help both parties win a successful contract, some will give advantage only to one side (and usually only in the short-term). When looking out for these techniques beware of various traps which can be set by the other party:

- Long speeches, which numb you into submission and hide the real objectives of the other party.

- Quick counter proposals which fool you into thinking the other party is making concessions and which may be used to get you to agree to something quickly.

- Loose words which appear to mean more than they actually give.

- Induced disagreement which leads you to question what you have said earlier through fallacious argument.

- A lack of any response, which may be designed to make you think that you are being totally unreasonable.

Preparing, planning and practising

You must decide what your best alternative to a negotiated agreement (BATNA) is. This may include what you can do if there is no contract.

You must then define the goal you are aiming to achieve through the negotiation. This is likely to be an agreement which satisfies everybody's interests, is amongst the best options available, is legitimate for both parties, is better than your BATNA, and includes commitments by both parties that are real and durable. Most importantly, you must be able to communicate your suggestions effectively so that the other party understands your position.

To do this you must do some preparation work. You must dig under the stated positions to find out the genuine interests of both parties. Then, thinking about these genuine interests, you must invent some options to maximise the gain for both parties. Then you must pick the best options and work on them to build legitimacy around the proposals. This means that the parties at the negotiations can sell them easily within their organisations.

For the negotiation itself you need to focus on the relationship, not just between your organisations, but between the individuals who are going to be present. Sometimes particular individuals have particular interests which must be satisfied. You must work out how you are going to communicate your proposals clearly, both at the negotiation and later to those who will be making the decision. This may mean putting your proposals in writing so that they can be reported back accurately after you have met face to face. It may mean preparing presentation materials or even a mock up of what you are offering.

You must try to understand the other party's BATNA and test this during the discussions. Is there a competitor waiting in the wings? Or is your offer by far the best the purchaser has received?

You should only commit yourself to an option when you have compared this to your BATNA and checked that it is better.

When it comes to preparing for the negotiation, you can never do too much. In an ideal world you would spend perhaps ten times as long on the preparation as you do in the negotiation itself. However, in real life it is unlikely you will have that long so you must use your time well.

When academics have researched the art of negotiation they have found that there is very little difference between effective negotiators and average negotiators, in terms of the amount of time spent planning, but there is a significant difference over the way the time is spent.

Effective negotiators, for example, consider a wider range of potential outcomes per issue than the average negotiator (typically 5 rather than 2.5). They also spend more time, approximately three times as much, considering areas of common ground where bridges of agreement can be built.

One significant difference which has been noticed is that average negotiators use sequence planning, in which they anticipate discussing item A, then B, then C, then D. Effective negotiators, however, are prepared to discuss the items in any order. They are not reliant upon their adversary meekly following their plan, but are fluid and flexible in their approach.

Planning for a negotiation should be a continual process. It is folly to have a large number of major contracts requiring re-negotiation within a short space of time. Far better to have them spread throughout the year and so avoid making time an additional pressure on the seller. All you need is some compliant customers!

Once a negotiation with a customer has finished, then is the time to start planning for the next one. Very few of us at the end of any task stand back and say 'How could I have done that job better?' In a negotiation, a post mortem or de-briefing session can be invaluable if recorded and used for the next contract negotiation. Buyers are particularly poor at recording outcomes.

Salesmen on the other hand will very often spend half an hour or so following a sales interview recording the meeting in a report. The detail included in these forms varies from company to company. Many will cover not merely the business that was conducted, but also what on the surface might appear to be superfluous details about the buyer, their interests, their pre-occupations, their personality, in some instances even their favourite lunchtime tipple.

There are two reasons for this post-interview de-briefing; one is that it is an investment. This is the time when details are freshest in your mind. It is far easier to review the significant points of a meeting immediately after that meeting than six months later. The personal details are important when you consider that companies don't negotiate, people do. A quotation by Sir Francis Bacon best summarises the logic of this: 'If you would work any man, you must either know his nature and fashions and so lead him; or his ends and so persuade him; or his weaknesses and disadvantages and so owe him; or those that have interest in him and so govern him.'

What preparation should you do?

Firstly, consider the alternatives available to everyone. Assess your BATNA and work on improving it. Estimate your customer's BATNA and consider ways in which that might be worsened.

Secondly, think about everybody's real interests. Identify and prioritise your own. Estimate and search out your customer's. Then define interests you have in common (which hopefully will be in the majority) and the conflicting interests.

Next look at the options available. This is where you must be creative. Invent as many mutual gain options as possible and identify how these meet both you and your customer's interests. Look for options which offer a high gain in return for a lowcost trade off.

Consider the legitimacy of your options. Research objective criteria such as the market rate, the norm for your industry, precedents for you and your customer and the history of your relationships. Think how and why a disinterested third party might decide to go for, or reject, a particular option.

Next work on the commitments expected from you and your customer. Identify the quality and substance of the commitments you want from the meeting you are preparing for and at the end of all the negotiations. Consider the authority of the people who will be present. Can they make the commitments you are seeking? Draft a framework agreement for both parties to sign on to at the end of the negotiation.

Think about the communication that will take place during the negotiation. Identify the information you will need to give, what you want to supply, what you want to obtain from your customer. Consider the purpose of that information, the people who will be supplying it, the form of the information and the process for obtaining it. There is little point in demanding information which serves little purpose and will require a great deal of effort to obtain.

Finally, consider your relationship with your customer. Define the current relationship between both your organisations and the individuals in each. Be realistic about the present situation. Visualise the desired relationship between you and plan to close the gap.

Having completed your preparation and planning try to practise the results before you meet your customer. To do this you need to find individuals who can take the role of your customer. These individuals must be independent from your team, and, ideally independent from your organisation, otherwise you may be lulled into a false sense of security. Brief them to take the customer's viewpoint and play the devil's advocate as much as possible. You need to have your ideas challenged, because this is what will happen in the real negotiation. Most organisations who

arrange realistic practise for their negotiations report improved results in the form of more profitable contracts. Indeed, one American defence equipment supplier believes they have increased their fees on government contracts by 12% as a result of using a devil's advocate approach to negotiation preparation.

Using successes and failures to improve hit rate

As with presentations make sure you take time after the negotiation to review your performance and the results. Whether you are successful in winning the contract or not consider what worked and what did not. Think about the reasons why you were successful or not, and use what works for you and your organisation to build on in the future. If your analysis indicates weaknesses in your technique seek appropriate training to improve. If there are weaknesses in the mix of your team, change this. Eliminate as many of the identified negative factors as possible and concentrate on the positive factors. Keep analysing the results to confirm whether you are making the right changes. If your hit rate remains the same reconsider your actions and try alternatives.

The legal issues

chapter 10

Chapter 10:
The legal issues

It is an unfortunate fact that the last thing most people involved in winning business for an organisation want to think about is the legal side of tendering. Legal terms and conditions are often seen as negatives, but this is precisely because they are there to protect you in case things go wrong.

Law of contract

Writing a tender is not often thought about in the same context as compiling a legal document but if the tender is used by your customer to define what is being supplied then the tender becomes part of the contract. The law of contract therefore becomes applicable.

Tender writers don't have to be legal experts but they have to be aware of the implications and know when to seek further advice. It is helpful to become aware of what contracts are, how contracts are formed and how they are discharged.

In essence, English contract law is quite simple, you make your bargain and you carry it out. If you fail, you compensate the other party for what they have lost.

Valid and void contracts

To be a valid contract in the UK any contract has to satisfy seven criteria. Some of these criteria reflect upon tender writing:

1. There must be an offer by one party and acceptance of it by the other

2. There must be an intention to create a legal relationship

3. Each party must have the legal capacity to make the contract

4. The consent must be legally obtained, not by duress for example

5. Consideration must be present, money must change hands

6. The law must not disapprove of the contract

7. The job must be possible.

The last is often very important to compilers of tenders. If the job is impossible to perform, maybe you are required to break fundamental laws of nature or attempt what is not possible to achieve, then the contract will be either void, voidable or

unenforceable. The impossibility may come from the customer's specification or by your own creation.

A void contract is one which doesn't exist in the eyes of the law, a voidable contract can be made void by any of the parties and an unenforceable contract is where there is no evidence of a contract being in place.

Implications on tenders

As a contract only exists when it has been unconditionally accepted, the tender when it forms part of the contract, must be clear, unambiguous, understandable and acceptable. If any part is such that the other party offers only a qualified acceptance, then there is no legal contract.

If your customer bases their purchasing documents on your tender, your tender must mean what it says, the words you use must convey exactly what you have in mind and exactly what you want to supply under your stipulated conditions.

If your proposed solution proves to be unattainable, then you risk the contract becoming unenforceable, or voidable depending upon the circumstances. A perfectly valid contract may be frustrated by a subsequent impossibility.

A further consideration is whether the tender has to be translated and what language is the definitive one. Even if the legal document is in English, the words should be chosen to facilitate translation; short sentences and short words help to prevent misunderstandings.

As with all legal matters, it is wise when confronted with a problem to take professional advice at an early stage. In most companies, there will be a responsible person to whom you can turn. Get to know them and ask for their advice readily.

Communication of offers and acceptances

A particularly critical time is when a contract is about to be placed. Exchanges of detailed information will only form part of the contract if they are submitted before the contract is formed. Offers and acceptances sent by letter are valid from the time of posting, not the time of receipt. By other means, such as e-mail, verbal, telephone or telex, they are valid from the time of receipt. Acceptance of course can be made by any means.

Withdrawal of an offer can again be made by any method of communication. It can be made by you at any time up to the point when your tender has been accepted by your customer but a withdrawal is valid at the time of receipt. If notices of acceptance and withdrawal cross in the post, you have a contract.

Discharge of contract

Generally this is only achieved by a precise and complete performance as described in the contract. Note that the word 'precise' means that you have to measure what is achieved and therefore your tender has to be capable of such interpretation.

Contracts which are not discharged, i.e. not completed, can be settled if suitable adjustments are agreed. Typically this could be part payment for the work completed, or your customer may deduct the cost of finishing the work properly from your account. If the work is substantially short, then any claim by you can be rejected by your customer.

Generally, negotiation between the parties is the normal course for settling a disputed finish to the contract, resort to arbitration is reserved for very difficult situations and the ultimate course of action, seeking legal redress, is avoided wherever possible.

Implied and express terms

There are two types of terms to a contract, expressed and implied. This subject of writing tenders has been primarily concerned with express terms, those which are clearly set out in the contract, those which the parties intend to be binding. Implied terms are those which are not written down in your contract.

Express terms

Expressed terms can be made orally or in writing, or a combination of these methods. Traditionally, expressed terms have been seen as either of two types and having varying degrees of importance. Conditions are terms which go to the essence of the contract and breach can lead to repudiation, with damages. Less serious are warranties where the only remedy is damages for loss.

There is a grey area between the two and certain sentences or clauses can fall into either category, depending on the contract. So the courts now tend to look at the effect of a breach of contract. If the effect is serious then the injured party can repudiate.

Implied terms

Implied terms are those not stated by the parties, but by law, are part of the contract. They include:

- terms implied by custom, as by the established practice or usage by trade

- terms implied by statute, civil law, Sales of Goods Act, etc.

- terms implied by the Courts, the doctrine of the implied term – the presumed intention.

Enforcement of contract

Legal remedies are designed to compensate the injured party, not to penalise the defaulter. Damages are payment to the injured party for failure to perform by the other party.

Liquidated damages are a genuine pre-estimate of the loss which could occur and they are written into the contract. The sum or sums have to be realistic otherwise they count as penalties, in which case the law will not enforce them. During the tendering phase of a project, you may choose to build into your price a contingency to cover the risk involved with the imposition of liquidated damages.

Unliquidated damages have no monetary values attributed to them in the contract. If a party thinks that they have been badly treated, they have to ask the court to assess the loss.

Both types of damages have the same principle applying to them, that is that individuals (companies) ought not to make a profit from damages. It is also the duty of an injured party to take all steps to mitigate their loss.

Sale of Goods Act 1979

Set down in this Act is a set of implied conditions to protect the buyer. Perhaps the most important for a tender writer is section 14.3 which states that '....the goods supplied under the contract are reasonably fit for the purpose....'

Primarily this was seen as protecting the consumer but it also protects the buyer in non-consumer sales. A supplier has to deliver goods to fit the customer's purpose, even if it has not been explicitly stated what is needed. However, if your customer has detailed specifically how he wants a task performed, he then has to carry some of the liability. It is a prudent buyer, therefore, who asks his customer to deliver a function, rather than specifying a detailed piece of equipment.

Transfer of ownership

It is important to consider and state when the title to (ownership of) your supplied goods will pass to the customer. There are many moments when transfer can take place and it is generally left to you to decide. Often this takes place on delivery, but it could take place after acceptance trials, after commissioning, or after a certain payment has been made for instance. The factors which will guide the decision are your cash flow, when payments will be made and whether they will be held up pending successful trials, and you also need to consider problems of insolvency of those around you. If you have delivered your equipment to your customer and they go broke, how will you reclaim your goods if they have not yet paid for them but they have the title to them?

Intellectual property rights

The term 'intellectual property' is given to the various laws which protect ideas and work derived from intellectual effort. Different types of creation have different types of protection lasting for different lengths of time.

The best way to keep a secret is not to tell anyone about it, however this is not always practical. If you have such proprietary information, define what it is and write an agreement around it. Breach of confidence can then be pursued through the courts.

Copyright protects your actual document from being copied, it doesn't protect the information in the document from being used in another form of words. Copyright is automatic but it is a wise move to state who owns the copyright of any document you would like to protect. Copyright now lasts for 70 years after the death of the author as a result of the EC Directive on Copyright Term.

A trademark is a name or a symbol, registration is optional. It doesn't protect the goods or the services, just the name or the logo. As long as you pay the renewal fees, you have protection. The Trade Marks Act 1984 in the UK implements the EU Trademarks Directive which extended the scope of trademarks to include geographical names and 'collective' marks, and simplified the process of registration throughout Europe.

Patent applications must pass a stringent test before being granted. The content of the application must be a new idea, must be novel, must be capable of application, must not break the laws of nature and must not be obvious to the average person with skill in the relevant field. Patents last for 20 years if, of course, the renewal fees are duly paid.

The Copyright, Designs and Patents Act of 1988 introduced the concept of Registered and Design Rights. Essentially, a Registered Design is for designs which appeal to the eye, have an aesthetic shape or a surface feature, whereas Design Rights apply to articles which have non-artistic shapes and manufactured articles.

A Registered Design lasts for 25 years and you need to apply to the Design Registry before you sell. It is intended to stop others from using similar designs. Design Rights last from 10 years from the first sale, or 15 years after recording the design. They are automatically granted and are intended to stop others from making your articles. However, this protection is partially waived in the last 5 years of the period and you cannot stop others from making your item but you can claim royalties.

Your drawings for manufactured articles not able to be registered continue to be covered by copyright but after 10 years the design can be copied (for instance by re-creating the drawing from the article). This affects the supply of spare parts for long life items.

EC regulations

Product liability

You are required to have duty of care for your product, such that it is inherently safe. This applies to all aspects: design, manufacture, materials, etc. If your proposed solution proves defective, you become liable.

In your defence you can take various measures to mitigate any future problems, however you cannot disclaim liability for death or personal injury caused by negligence. One of the measures is to try to pass on to your suppliers or subcontractors a share of the risk, by asking them for an indemnity. Sometimes the law will encourage this, as illustrated by section 6 of the Health and Safety at Work Act.

Other measures are continually to strive for excellence, disclaim liability wherever lawful, review insurance cover and, as mentioned before, talk to your legal department at an early stage.

European Standards

The European Commission wants to see trade barriers removed and wants to arrive at a position of open trading and open tendering. To achieve this they have decreed that standards shall be harmonised and that Member States must recognise the standards that goods are made to.

Three standards setting organisations, CEN (The European Committee for Standardisation), CENELEC (The European Committee for Electrotechnical Standards) and ETSI (The European Telecommunications Standards Institute) work with the national standards bodies of the member states, BSI in the case of the UK, to produce Harmonised European Standards. These are given 'EN' numbers. The European Standards are then transcribed into identically worded national standards. Typically, the well-known Quality Management Standard BS 5750 is derived from EN 29000, not only derived from but also using the very same words. In turn, this provided the draft for the International Standard ISO 9001, by which this standard is generally currently known.

When tenders are being produced, therefore, it is sensible to refer to the European Standard that you are using. Not only does this show that you are aware of the importance of tendering in Europe, but when tendering to a European partner, the tender assessors can recognise and understand the EN number immediately.

The Single European Market

The 'Single European Act' committed the European Commission to establish a single market by 31 December 1992. The single market is described as '...an area without internal frontiers, with free movement of goods, persons and capital...' Trade barriers have come down and much red tape has been cut.

The key decision making body in Europe is the Council of Ministers. They issue:

- **Regulations** – these become immediately binding and the relevant European law supersedes national laws.

- **Directives** – these must be transposed into national law within a prescribed time period.

- **Decisions** – these become binding only when transposed into national law.

- **Recommendations** – these set out policies.

Directives tend to be the main vehicle for affecting the new ways business must be conducted. There are a whole variety of them, many covering safety and others covering the way public purchasing is to be carried out. These latter directives are represented by the Supplies Directive, the Works Directive, the Services Directive and the Utilities Directive.

All these directives lay down similar rules and the ones governing public purchasing are on the basis of the best value for money.

The Supplies Directive covers the supply of goods to central, regional and local government, the Works Directive applies to the same bodies for building and civil

engineering work, while the Services Directive applies to all other contracts for these bodies. The Utilities Directive covers the provision of supplies, works and services to public and private purchasers in the energy, water, transport and telecommunications sectors.

Tendering in Europe

Before producing tenders for European customers, there are a few aspects that are worth considering to help ensure success:

- Are you familiar with the rules? Familiarity with the Directives will help you prepare bids and develop new and existing markets.

- Determine who the new customers are, and who the new competitors will be – assess their strengths and weaknesses.

- Check that your products and services are suitable for the new locality. Do your products match the needs of the local market?

- Are you using European Standards? Are there any unofficial local standards recognised, such as ones set by the local market leader?

- Is your company properly organised and trained?

- Is your sales literature properly translated? Do your tenders need to be presented in the local language? Do you need to redesign the sales literature to suit local needs?

The impact of TUPE

The Transfer of Undertakings (Protection of Employment) Regulations 1981 must be considered when offering service contracts. These regulations implement the European Directive on Acquired Rights. The Directive was updated in 1998 and the UK Regulations are being amended yet again. They are fraught with difficulties as tenderers are caught in crossfire between the UK Government and the European Commission over whether the Directive has been correctly implemented and it is essential that tenderers and customers alike consult an employment lawyer if they are in any doubt whether they are covered. The rules are of particular significance to any tenderer aiming to take over any public sector services, whether from local or central government. They will also have to be considered by any company offering facilities management services. Secondary transfers, those where an initial outsourcing contract has reached its end and a new competition has been organised to continue the service for the next period, are also caught by this legislation.

Basically the rules state that if you take over a separate undertaking, with or without assets, the staff involved effectively have their contracts of employment transferred and are treated as if they had worked for you for as long as they had been working for the undertaking taken over. Their terms of employment can be altered only in minor respects – they must remain substantially the same. However, there was one exception – pension provisions are not carried across and the transferred staff will normally simply join the successful tenderer's normal pension scheme. Even here, proposed revisions to the legislation require the new pension scheme to offer substantially the same benefits as the old one.

The determination of what constitutes an undertaking should be a matter of fact – but this is where the complications set in. It is not necessary for the transferred business to be a separate limited company, or for it to have profit as an aim. Probably any section which has its own budget and identifiable staff will constitute an undertaking.

Electronic tendering

PITFALLS FOR THE UNWARY

THE WAY AHEAD

chapter 11

Chapter 11:
Electronic tendering

Increasingly these days you will find yourself using electronics for part of the tender process. The notices for forthcoming contracts in the European public sector and utilities are now only published electronically in their original form, although several paper publications reprint selected parts of selected notices. To be sure of not missing any opportunities in this area you need to access these notices. Purchasers in these areas and others are increasingly joining electronic 'exchanges' and are encouraging their suppliers to do likewise. They intend to advertise their requirements in these marketplaces and use them to receive tenders back. The problem at the time of writing is that there are so many exchanges that all but the most specialist suppliers and contractors must consider joining many and it is far from clear what the cost structure will be. Many purchasers are setting up exchanges in the belief they can make a great deal of money through subscriptions and transaction fees. The more enlightened are approaching the exchanges as a way of reducing transaction costs for all parties.

Some purchasers are now placing their enquiry documents on websites so that tenderers can access the documents easily and quickly. Others will send out documents on CD-ROMs or disks. Sometimes the documents have to be returned in paper form, but increasingly purchasers are requesting tenders in electronic format. This at present usually takes the form of returning a disk or disks in a sealed envelope, along with paper documents. The envelopes will then be opened in the same way as other tenders.

Sometimes you may be asked to submit prices by e-mail, but this is usually only for simpler items or low-value items.

Purchasers use the electronic form of tenders to help them analyse your bid against your competitors, so to avoid upsetting your customer you must stick to the format requested. If this presents you with a problem make sure you discuss how to overcome this with your customer well before the final deadline.

Pitfalls for the unwary

As you may guess, with such a proliferation of electronic methods there is a problem with standards. Even the simplest of tenders require word-processor formats that can be read by the other party. In theory this is easy to achieve, but in practice, many find it very difficult to remember to save back to the agreed format. For more complex documents, containing drawings or pictures, the potential problems multiply because the text may be readable at the other end, but not the drawing. The result is a potentially unsuccessful tender. It is therefore very important to consider the other party's requirements for formats.

There is also a lot of concern about the security of electronic tendering. One problem is that electronic documents are so easily copied. This may be done by a disgruntled employee in your organisation or a 'plant' put there by your competitor. Of course, there is nothing inherently different to the security needed when producing traditional paper tenders, but too often security is more lax because people find it more difficult to understand what it is necessary to do to maintain security.

E-mails must always be regarded as an unreliable medium. They can be intercepted, they can end up in the wrong address or they can end up at no address at all. The slightest incorrect character in the address will cause the e-mail not to arrive at its intended destination. There is no human to correct minor mistakes in addressing, as there is with paper. However, e-mails are fast and can travel half way around the world in less than a few seconds. E-mails can also be mislaid when they do arrive at their destination and their contents are immediately visible. One way to get round this problem is to send your tender as an attachment, but that carries difficulties of its own. E-mails are a known source of computer viruses and in order to limit the threat many companies strip off all attachments as soon as they enter their internal systems. This makes electronic tendering using e-mail more difficult than it should be.

Tendering electronically is perfectly valid in the UK, but there may be hidden difficulties aside from the technology when submitting tenders to other countries. Sometimes a tender has to be both signed and sealed to be legally valid. In these cases it is necessary to use the electronic equivalent of both a signature and a seal when submitting your tender. This usually means that you need to use some special form of software which allows these additional security measures, along the lines of existing EDI systems.

Obviously, it is good to please your customers but when they demand so many different technical solutions to electronic tendering it may be necessary to take a step back to check that you are not pouring money into systems which will only suit a minority of your customers. Over the years, many computer systems

suppliers have offered the holy grail of a single solution which fits all, but nearly all have been found wanting in practice. The technology in this area is developing so fast, that a common solution may not be far away, but it is not there yet. Of course, if your customers are nearly all in a particular industry the proprietary solution required may not be a problem because it suits most of the others as well but remember that it may limit your ability to tender electronically to other customers in other industries in the future.

The way ahead

There is little doubt in my mind that electronic tendering will become much more common in the future. Tendering electronically should help reduce the costs of the transactions and there will be some timesavings, although the bulk of the time needed to write a tender will remain the same. However, electronic documents will help you get the required information as quickly as possible to your subcontractors and partners and in as complete a form as possible and should help you integrate their responses into your master tender.

The use of electronic signatures, seals and locks will become more commonplace. This means you will be able to send a secure tender, knowing that it cannot be opened until the due time for opening, when the customer will be able to access all the bids simultaneously. The systems should be able to send you an acknowledgement that your tender has arrived even though it may not be opened until a later time. You can then be reassured that your hard work has arrived at its destination.

It is also possible that standardised formats for enquiry and tender information will be produced. Each piece of information will be given a standard structure. You may be able to prepare a lot of standard information about your organisation in advance. The purchaser will be able to reassemble the pieces in the order that suits them. This will again save time and therefore reduce costs.

To some extent these standards will be introduced through the electronic commerce exchanges being set up to serve particular industries. The key will be whether the different industries' requirements can come together.

Perfect your tenders

chapter 12

Chapter 12:
Perfect your tenders

This Report should have given you some ideas for improving your tenders. In many cases, it may simply have confirmed that you are, indeed, doing the right thing at present. But you do need to be aware of how successful your tendering is. Then you can work out what to improve and how.

Review of actions to improve your proposals

You must first of all be aware of what works for your organisation and what does not. To do this you must keep a record of your tenders, what you bid for, what you declined, who won each bid, the price bid, and so on. A simple format for tender records is included as Appendix 3 (page 122) to this Report. You need to keep your record under review at regular intervals and be particularly alert for any indication that you are becoming less successful.

One principle to remember is that if something works for you and your organisation, think very hard before changing it. If you have hit on a winning formula, stick with it. Only try to change those aspects which are not successful, or which are required to deal with changing circumstances such as technological advances, new competitors, new opportunities and so on.

It is useful to have a checklist of actions and contents to ensure nothing is forgotten in the heat of the moment of producing a tender, when time is limited and you are under great pressure. The following examples give you an idea of the type of checklist you may need, but you should produce your own items to suit the particular circumstances of your organisation. Note that the order is not significant here. Put yours into an order of importance to your organisation, but remember this may change from one tender to another and from one customer to another.

CHAPTER 12: PERFECT YOUR TENDERS

Key points for good tenders

Good tenders will:

- mean good business – the best business, not just the dregs

- have a greater chance of success

- lower your risk and financial exposure

- be fully read by the assessor

- reduce the customer's tendency to add extras and contingencies to your price to cover unknowns

- satisfy the buyer's needs

- demonstrate that you are serious and that you are putting in the 'A' team

- help the buyer to sell *your* tender upwards, for example to his board

- strengthen your hand in negotiations

- protect your company

A good tender:

- states the requirements

- proves compliance

- describes the extras

- justifies costs

- explains the conditions

- instils confidence in you and creates credibility

- reduces your risk (whilst it appears to reduce your customer's risk)

- reduces your customer's workload

- keeps your managers alert for new ideas etc.

- introduces innovations in a careful and controlled fashion.

110

Key points on European regulations

- Europe presents opportunities for you to expand your business

- Directives cover building, construction and civil engineering schemes, supplies of materials and the buying of services

- Local and Central Government and utility companies have to advertise their contracts (if over certain limits) in Europe

- The thresholds for advertising contracts in the three areas are reviewed every few years and are subject to change

- Advertisements appear daily in the *Official Journal* and the TED data bank

- Timescales differ for each method of tendering

- There are areas where a public body is not required to tender

- The Government rely on you as a contractor to act as a watchdog – report any deviations from the rules to the Department of the Environment, Transport and the Regions or the Department of Trade and Industry.

Key points about deciding to bid

- Make sure you fully understand the requirements

- Is the job part of your normal business, or part of your corporate plan for expansion?

- Do you have the capability to do the job technically, with the right resources and in the timescale?

- Is the risk acceptable to your organisation?

- Can you offer a compliant solution?

- Is the customer financially sound and creditworthy?

- Do you know the customer, their organisation, and the key decision-makers?

- Have you influenced the specification, and if so, does it favour you?

- Do you know what the customer's preferred solution is? Are you able to play it back to them?

- Are you able to meet the customer's commercial conditions adequately?

Key points about tender preparation

- Can you influence the specification? If 'yes', then do it to your advantage

- Try to design out weaknesses, or at least minimise their effects

- Be aware of the competition – work out their strengths, weaknesses and strategies

- Give the customer a 'good listening to'

- Ensure traceability between the different sections

- Ensure your basic offer is compliant and prove it with facts and figures

- Play back the preferred solution

- Make a claim, then prove it

- Quote the full price for a mandatory requirement and the lowest price for a target specification

- Make a review timetable, and stick to it.

Key points to help you write effective, selling tenders

- Always consider your reader, lighten their load, make their life easier

- If your words can be misinterpreted, they will – to *your* disadvantage

- Keep it simple and you'll keep the reader's interest

- Keep it logical, make your words and ideas flow

- Don't be proud, listen to advice, and take constructive criticism in the manner it should be given

- Get your spelling and punctuation right – every time

- Put the key point of a paragraph in the first sentence

- Know when to use *shall* and *will*

- Never use slang and avoid jargon wherever you can

- Watch out for American jargon, unless you are selling to an American customer, avoid it at all times

- Beware of the perils of word processors

- But after all this – don't follow the rules of English slavishly, break a rule occasionally rather than convey the wrong meaning.

Key points you must remember when putting it all together

- Say what you mean, and mean what you say

- Always be 'accurate'

- Make sure your bid is complete, use checklists and other methods to help

- Be consistent, don't contradict yourself in various parts of the document

- Don't be ambiguous, be precise with your words

- Make sure what you are saying and proposing is relevant

- Be adequate, don't overdesign, and don't gild the lily

- Be thorough, don't be vague – vagueness will be marked down

- Make sure your offer and your words are effective

- Try always to be watertight, use proper construction and plug all the holes

- Watch out for trade names, use them sensibly

- Use commercial alternatives where you can.

Key points to do with publishing

- The tender document is a reflection of your company, you'll be judged by it

- Keep all graphics, drawings, photographs, tables etc. the right way up – so the assessor doesn't have to turn the page to see them

- Keep charts and drawings within all the margins

- Add pizzazz, but use it with restraint

- Use an Executive Summary, in one form or another

- Include a message from your MD for new customers and significant jobs

- Always address technical, management and commercial matters separately

- Consider your reader, make their reading task easy

- Include a Glossary for jargon and abbreviations you use

- Put specialised technical descriptions and dissertations into appendices.

Key points for presentations

- Establish your customer's objectives

- Establish the time frame

- Find out who will be in your customer's team

- Decide on the key points you want to make

- Decide on your approach

- Maintain discipline in your team

- Maintain your customer's interest

- Rehearse, and rehearse again

- Plan the administration.

Key points for negotiations

Pre-negotiation

- Make effective use of planning time

- Set objectives in a band

- Aim high but be credible

- Search for variances and be flexible

- Remember your strengths.

Face to face

- Establish their wants

- Look and listen for signals

- Stick to common ground.

Post negotiation

- Record, publish and implement the agreement

- Debrief your team.

Key points on the legal issues

You need to be certain that:

- Your offer is possible and legal

- Your tender is clear and unambiguous so that it can be accepted simply, with no quarrels

- You have recorded the despatch of your offer

- You have avoided pseudo legal words and phrases

- You have understood the implications of any liquidated damages clauses

- You have avoided any restrictive practices

- You have decided the best time to transfer the title of the goods

- You understand what Implied Terms are relevant

- You have taken all steps to reduce your product liability

- You have taken into account the Intellectual Property Rights issues

- You have addressed the relevant environmental aspects.

Key points for electronic tendering

Have you:

- Checked all information sources on the Internet?

- Joined the relevant trading exchanges?

- Established electronic signatures?

- Returned a disk if requested?

- Kept to required document formats?

- Ensured your customer can read special formats?

- Installed appropriate security measures?

- Used appropriate security measures?

- Used the right signatures and locks?

- Used any published standard formats for tenders?

Appendices

Appendix 1:
Common Estimating Procedure (Engineering)

ESTIMATE SUMMARY	Operating Company		Estimator					*Signature of Authorised Management*
	Division							
Customer		Date	Base Dates					
Project Title		Time	for Recoveries					
Project Number		Revision	for Merchant A/c					

#	Designation					Total	% of CV	*Proposal Manager*
0	Total Hours							
0.0	Average Hourly Rates							
1.1	Project Management hours							
1.2	Engineering hours							
1.3	Works Conversion hours							
1.4	Training hours							
1.5	Supervision of Erection hours							
1.6	Supervision of Commissioning hours							*Estimating Manager*
1.7	Construction Site Management hours							
1.8	Direct Hire Labour hours							
1.9								
1.10	Indirect Overhead							
1.11	Adjustment, Levy							
1.12	Escalation							
1	Total Recoveries hours							

2.1	In-house Design Equipment						*Sales Director*
2.2	Factory/Works purchases						
2.3	Bought out equipment						
2.4	Electric/instruments/autom. equipment						
2.5	Nominated vendors						
2.6	Spares						
2.7	Packaging and Freight						
2.8	Subcontracted engineering						
2.9	Construction						*Divisional Director*
2.10	Specialist supervision						
2.11	Subcontracted training						
2.12	Travel and subsistence						
2.13	Site expenses						
2.14	Other Expenses (training, prints, etc.)						
2.15							
2.16							
2.17	Escalation						
2	**Total Merchant Account**						

#						
3.1	Royalties and Licenses					
3.2	Commissions					
3.3	Taxes, Duties and Permits					
3.4	Finance for cash flow					
3.5	Insurances					
3.6	Bonds					
3.7	Financing					
3.8	NCM, COFACE, HERMES, EXIM etc.					
3.9						
3	**Total other costs**					
	Total external costs (2+3) **Total base estimate (1+2+3)**					
4	Risk provision (Rc)					
	Total costs (1+2+3+4)					
5.1	Net profit pre-interest					
5.2	Net profit post-interest					
6	**Contract Value (CV)**					
7	**Negotiating Margin**					
8	**Current Bid Price**					

Engineering/ Operations Director

Managing Director

Currency

Exchange Rate

Firm, Fixed or Budget

Tender validity:

Key schedules dates:

Total added value (1+5.2)

Appendix 2:
Risk factors in practice

Ex post attribution of factors responsible for schedule slip in World Bank supported power generation projects approved 1965-1986.

THERMAL POWER PROJECTS	
Responsible party or factor	**Specific factor or event**
Client/engineer	Legal requirements/bureaucratic procedure for awarding contracts
	Initial schedule was too optimistic
	Bid evaluation difficulties
	Delays in procurement/placement of orders
	Change in project scope
	Modifications to major equipment required
	Disagreement between bank and borrower over contract award
	Site change
Contractor/supplier	Labour disputes/strikes in manufacturer's country
	Labour disputes/strikes in project country
	Shipping delays due to oil crisis
	Substandard work had to be redone
	Equipment failure during testing
	Skilled labour shortage
	Manufacturing difficulties
	Shortage of materials
	Contractor inefficiency/lack of co-ordination
	Technical problems with equipment
	Contractor bankruptcy
	Transportation difficulties
Uncontrollable events	Damage/need to redesign civil works due to earthquake or other natural disaster
	Unusually bad weather
	Accident – damage to equipment
	Political turmoil/coup/invasion
	Civil disturbance

HYDRO-ELECTRIC POWER PROJECTS	
Responsible party or factor	**Specific factor or event**
Client/engineer	Initial schedule was too optimistic
	Geological problems
	Financial difficulties/tariff implementation problems
	Inefficient project management/ institutional weakness
	Design changes
	Change in project scope
	Relocation problems
	Delay in award of contracts/bid evaluation difficulties
	Design faults
	Procurement delays/difficulties
	Site change
	Land acquisition/site access problems
	Communication problems
	No bids received due to working conditions
	Major currency devaluation threatened project viability
	Project sponsors backed out
	Legal problems/delay in settling claims
	World-wide inflation
Contractor/supplier	Contractor bankruptcy
	Contractor inefficiency/inexperience/ incompetence
	Delays in shipping/delivery of equipment/transportation difficulties
	Substandard work had to be redone
	Shortage of materials
	Manufacturing difficulties
	Damage to equipment/dam or tunnel collapse
	Water infiltration/pressure damage
	Fire
	Equipment failure during testing
	Labour disputes/strikes in manufacturer's country
	Fuel shortage
	Labour disputes/strikes in project country
	Communication problems
	Skilled labour shortage
	Change in contractors
	Legal problems/delay in settling claims
Uncontrollable events	Landslides/mudslides/rockfalls
	Unusually bad weather
	Political turmoil/coup/invasion/war
	Flood damage
	Earthquake

121

Appendix 3:
Bid registration system

Customer: _____Source: _____

Enquiry Date: _____Tender Due: _____Contract to be let: _____

Project Title: _____Enquiry Ref: _____

Brief Description: _____

_____

_____

_____

Value to Org.: _____Probability: _____Cost of Tender: _____

Known Competition: _____

_____

_____

Priority: _____Development needed: Y/N   Development Cost: _____

Resources required: _____

Person/Days: _____Costs: _____
(detail on attached sheet as required)

Bid/No Bid Approved:_____Date: _____

Bid Preparation

Bid Manager:_____

Bid Section: _____

Other Departments: _____

_____

_____

Bid Review Date:_____Location:_____

Result

Who Won? Us/ _____ Nearest Competitor: _____

Reasons for Win/Lose: _____

_____

_____

Customer's Reaction to Our Bid: _____

_____

_____

Suggested Improvements: _____

_____

_____

_____